The Health Insurance Answer Book

CHARLES E. VADAKIN II
Union Mutual Life Insurance Company
ZELDA LIPTON
Union Mutual Life Insurance Company

Institute For Management
Division of Panel Publishers, Inc.

Library of Congress Cataloging-in-Publication Data
Vadakin, Charles E.
The health insurance answer book.

1. Insurance, Health—United States—Handbooks, manuals, etc. I. Lipton, Zelda. II. Title.
HG9396.V33 1986 368.3′82′00973 86-18648
ISBN 0-916592-67-7

by
PANEL PUBLISHERS, INC.
A Member of the Worldwide Wolters Samsom Group
14 Plaza Road
Greenvale, New York 11548

Printed in the United States of America

How to Use The Health Insurance Answer Book

Group health insurance is one of the most important aspects of an employer's total compensation strategy. It is the foundation of a company's employee benefits plan and provides essential financial protection for employees against catastrophic health care expenses.

In deciding on a group health insurance plan, an employer faces many issues. The key decisions that must be made include:

- Whom to work with in designing and purchasing a plan;
- What benefits to provide;
- How much to spend;
- How to fund the plan costs;
- What cost-control mechanisms to implement; and
- How to deal with ongoing administration.

This book is designed to answer the questions surrounding these basic decisions. It covers only the health care and group health insurance portions of the employee benefits package, since these areas are among the most complex and costly.

Although health insurance is often defined to include coverage for disability, accidental death, and dental care, the questions and answers in this text deal almost exclusively with medical care insurance. Other coverages are addressed only when it is necessary to explain their interrelationship with medical care in a total benefits package.

►**Organization of the Book:** The book is divided into 10 chapters, which are intended to take the reader from the fundamental concepts of group insurance through the selection and buying process, ending with a discussion of future trends in health care. The questions are numbered in a consecutive sequence (1–421) through the book.

►**Listing of Questions:** The list of questions in the front of the book helps the readers locate areas of immediate interest. A short summary of each chapter heads each section of the listing. This is followed by all the questions that are answered in that chapter—with each question identified by a question number and referred to the page number on which it appears. Thus, the reader can easily locate an area of interest and the specific questions relating to it.

►**Appendix:** The Appendix consists of statistical tables that plainly show the increase in health care costs in different regions of the country.

►**List of State Insurance Commissioners:** The names, addresses, telephone numbers, and office hours of the Commissioners of Insurance are included in a state-by-state listing from the American Council of Life Insurance.

►**Glossary of Acronyms:** A glossary of acronyms is included to help explain the many abbreviated terms that are frequently used in the health care industry. The acronyms are arranged in alphabetical order.

►**Index:** At the back of the book, there is a traditional topical index as a further aid to locating specific information. All references in the index are to question numbers rather than page numbers.

This question-and-answer format offers a clear and useful guide to understanding the complex, but extremely important, area of health insurance.

About the Authors

CHARLES E. VADAKIN II is Vice President of Union Mutual Life Insurance Company, where he is in charge of the Flexible Benefits Division. Previously, he served as Vice President, Group Life/Medical Products, and Second Vice President, Human Resources. He received a B.S. in physics and mathematics from Davis and Elkins College, and a Masters in Aerospace Operations Management from the University of Southern California. He is a veteran of the United States Air Force and presently serves in the United States Air Force Reserve with the rank of Lieutenant Colonel. Mr. Vadakin has spoken before many insurance industry groups, including the Employers Council on Flexible Compensation and the Risk Insurance Management Society.

ZELDA LIPTON is Second Vice President, Flexible Benefits Division, Union Mutual Life Insurance Company. Previously, she served as Second Vice President, Group Life/Medical Products, and has held a number of product development and research positions in the insurance industry over the course of her 20-year career. She received a B.A. from Hunter College, and an M.A. from New York University. She is a Fellow of the Life Management Institute, a member of the Governor's Certificate of Need Advisory Council for the State of Maine, and appears in *Who's Who in American Women.* Ms. Lipton is a contributing author to *A Course in Group Life and Health Insurance,* published by the Health Insurance Association of America, and *The Handbook of Employee Benefits: Designing Funding and Administration,* published by Dow Jones-Irwin.

Table of Contents

Listing of Questions

An Overview of Group Insurance

Group insurance is a technique for providing essential protection against financial loss resulting from death, disability, or significant illness or injury. This chapter describes the different types of group insurance available, the various ways in which employers purchase it, and the development and growth of the concept of group health insurance.

Choosing an Intermediary

Because of limited resources and a lack of expertise, most small employers use an insurance professional—either an agent, broker, or consultant—to assist in the design, purchase, and administration of a group health insurance plan. This chapter examines the various types of professionals and the services they offer.

Factors Influencing the Design of Group Health Insurance Plans

A variety of federal and state laws regulate the group health insurance market. These governmental factors, as well as important social and financial considerations, will strongly influence an employer's decision-making process. This chapter covers both the external and internal factors that affect the basic decisions concerning an employer's group health insurance plan. These statutes include state and federal laws like Medicare, ADEA, and ERISA, as well as requirements concerning size, eligibility, and participation in group health insurance plans.

Types of Health Insurance Plans and Benefits

With hundreds of insurance companies offering group health insurance plans, it is often difficult for smaller employers to determine exactly which plan will best meet their business objectives and their employees' health care needs. This chapter examines the different types of plans available and what benefits they provide.

Managing Health Insurance Costs

As health insurance costs have increased in recent years, insurers have redesigned their plans to include cost-containment features. This chapter explores the reasons behind rising health care costs and explains what some of these cost-containment features are and how they work.

Alternative Health Care Systems

The preceding chapter discusses ways to manage health care costs by adding plan design features such as second surgical opinions, outpatient surgery incentives, and utilization review. These approaches encourage more responsible health care consumption by consumers. Another cost-management option available to employers is to reorganize the way in which their employees' health care services are provided and paid for. This chapter discusses alternative health care delivery and reimbursement systems such as health maintenance organizations and preferred provider organizations.

Flexible Benefits

As the name denotes, flexible benefits plans come in all shapes to meet the needs of employees with diverse life styles and employers with varied objectives. This chapter covers the basic principles involved in the design and handling of flexible benefits plans, with emphasis on cafeteria plans as provided for under Section 125 of the Internal Revenue Code. These plans are new to the marketplace and promise to meet the needs of a changing work force, while providing a cost-management tool to employers.

Plan Rating and Funding

Plan rating and funding are important aspects of group health insurance. The approach used is the basis on which the cost of the plan to the employer is determined. This chapter covers plan rating and funding techniques, including conventional funding, high self-insured plans, deferred premium, retrospective premium arrangements, reserve reduction arrangements, minimum premium, pooling, experience rating, stop-loss insurance, and self-funding.

Group Health Insurance Plan Administration

Proper administration of the health insurance plan is essential if the employer and employee are to receive maximum value. Plan administration begins before the effective date of the plan and continues throughout the plan year and during the renewal period. This chapter examines plan administration and covers such topics as employee enrollment, claims filing, billing procedures, and the renewal process.

Future Trends in Health Insurance

Previous chapters addressed alternatives available to employers in such areas as design, cost management, funding, and administration of group health insurance plans. However, we are living in a very dynamic society, especially when it comes to health care and employee benefits. An employer that wants its employees to receive the greatest value for benefits dollars spent should be monitoring the developments in these fields and deciding when it makes sense to take advantage of them. This chapter discusses those trends that are likely to have an impact on employee benefits packages in the future.

An Overview of Group Insurance

Group insurance is a technique for providing essential protection against financial loss resulting from death, disability, or significant illness or injury. This chapter describes the different types of group insurance available, the various ways in which employers purchase it, and the development and growth of the concept of group health insurance.

-1-

What is group insurance?

Group insurance is an economical way to insure a group of individuals under a single contract, or policy, from financial loss resulting from illness, injury, or death. The contract is between the insurer and the entity representing the group—the policyholder. The group must be associated with the policyholder for some purpose other than the purchase of insurance. One set of premium rates for the entire group is determined by averaging the demographic characteristics such as age and sex for all individuals in the group.

-2-

How did group insurance originate?

Group insurance originated at the turn of the century in response to employers that wanted to provide employees with predetermined survivor benefits for their families in the event the employees died. In 1910, Montgomery Ward & Company, Inc., sought to purchase life insurance protection for its employees in mass quantity. At first, none of the major insurance companies was willing to sell a group policy that would insure all employees, regardless of health. Then, in 1911, The Equitable Life Assurance Society of the United States agreed to underwrite the group. By applying the economies of volume purchasing to the procurement of insurance, Montgomery Ward is credited with initiating the development of group insurance, although its policy was not the first actually written. In less than a decade, the soundness of group insurance was well-established in this country.

-3-

Is group insurance available only to single employers?

No. While the policyholder under group insurance is most often a single employer (corporation, partnership, or sole proprietorship), it can also be an entity such as a union or a professional association. In addition, a single group policy may be issued to cover employees of a number of different employers. These group insurance vehicles are often used to insure individuals who are employed by companies too small to offer group coverage on their own.

-4-

What is a multiple employer trust?

Under a multiple employer trust (MET), many small employers in the same or a related industry participate in a group plan under a trust arrangement. The trust, rather than each participating employer, is the policyholder, and the master contract is issued to a trustee. Through mass purchasing, small employers can afford a level of insurance benefits that is normally available only to larger employers. METs are most common among employers with 10 or fewer employees, but some trusts also offer coverage to larger groups.

-5-

How can a labor union provide group insurance?

A labor union can provide group insurance for its members under a policy issued to the union. The union is the policyholder, just as the trust is the policyholder under a MET. A union may purchase a group policy for a large number of members who are employed at one or several locations of the same company, or for union members working for different companies. Group insurance purchased through a union is particularly advantageous in industries like construction, where union members may work for many employers during a year.

Despite the opportunity for labor unions to purchase group insurance, few group contracts are issued to unions today. Organized labor more often obtains insurance benefits for its members through collective bargaining with employers. As a result, union members are usually covered under group insurance policies where they work.

-6-

What is an association plan?

A professional or trade association can provide coverage for its members or member companies under a policy issued to the association. The association is the policyholder. Examples of association groups include the National Teachers Association, the American Medical Association, and the New England Small College Association.

When compared with group employer plans, the percentage of eligible association members who actually enroll in these plans is usually small, because many association members have access to other insurance that may be less expensive or provide better coverage.

-7-

How prevalent is group insurance in the United States?

According to the Health Insurance Association of America, at the end of 1982, eight out of ten Americans were covered by group health insurance.

-8-

How else do Americans receive health insurance protection?

Besides participating in group insurance plans, Americans may also be covered under federal and state government-sponsored programs such as Medicare and Medicaid, service-type plans such as Blue Cross/Blue Shield, and individually purchased insurance policies. The chapter entitled "Alternative Health Care Systems" explains health maintenance organization (HMO) plans—another alternative to traditional group health insurance.

-9-

What is the major difference between group and individual insurance?

To purchase individual insurance, a person must generally provide evidence of insurability to the insurance company through health questionnaires and medical examinations. An insurer may decline coverage on the basis of the applicant's personal habits, health, medical history, age, income, or any other factors that come to bear on risk acceptance. Or the insurer may issue a policy with limitations on coverage.

Most group insurance, however, is issued without medical examination or other evidence of individual insurability because the insurer knows that it can cover enough individuals to balance those in poor health against those in good health. The risk of an insurer failing to achieve this balance is diminished as it underwrites additional group policies.

-10-

What is risk?

The risk an insurance company assumes when it agrees to cover a particular group is the possibility that claims will exceed the expected level. It is the chance of financial loss inherent in the group. Insurance companies use it to determine whether they will underwrite an insurance policy on a particular group.

The spread of risk is necessary not only because of the *expected* variations in a population's health but also because some policyholders—particularly very small groups—purchase group insurance to cover certain individuals with known health problems. This is a more costly way to obtain coverage for those high-risk individuals, but often the only way possible, given the evidence-of-insurability requirement for individual policies.

-11-

What is a group health insurance underwriter?

A group health insurance underwriter is a risk evaluator, in that he or she analyzes each individual group to determine the financial risk it represents for the insurance company. To determine the acceptability of the risk a particular group represents, the underwriter examines the composition of the group as it relates to age, sex, prior claims experience, and the desired plan design.

A recent trend in risk evaluation is "life-style analysis." The underwriter may take into account the number of smokers in a group, for example. If the group is an "acceptable risk," the underwriter then determines what limits should be set on coverage for the group and what prices the group should be charged. A group will be deemed an acceptable risk if it has characteristics that the underwriter feels can be accurately priced to reflect the risk to the insurance company. This price, or "quote," is provided to the group representative for delivery to the prospective policyholder.

-12-

What is antiselection?

Antiselection, or adverse selection, is the tendency for persons with known health problems to elect more insurance than healthy persons. These individuals as a group incur significantly greater health care expenses.

-13-

What are the advantages of group insurance vs. individual insurance?

For an employer that intends to provide insurance protection to its employees, the group approach ensures that all employees, regardless of health, can be covered. Those with known health problems, who might otherwise be unable to obtain individual insurance, can be covered automatically upon employment without evidence of insurability. Although some limits may be imposed on new hires for certain conditions that predated their enrollment in the plan, most employees can receive coverage as soon as they are eligible.

Group insurance offers a lower cost per unit of protection than individual insurance, because of the economies of scale resulting from selling, installing, and servicing one plan covering many individuals. In addition group plans are typically more flexible and progressive than individual coverage.

-14-

Why do most employers provide group health insurance?

Group insurance benefits have become a traditional and expected part of an employee's compensation and an integral part of an employer's total compensation strategy. A comprehensive benefits package allows employers to attract and retain quality employees. In markets in which certain skills are in short supply, employers often vie for labor by offering more attractive employee benefits plans than the competition.

In addition, group insurance is a concrete way for employers to show concern for their employees' welfare. For many employees, group protection is their only form of insurance protection; without it, they would be susceptible to financial catastrophe from the expenses associated with a major injury or prolonged disability. By giving employees the peace of mind that comes from knowing that they and their families are protected against financial hardship, group insurance enhances employee morale. A formal benefits program, therefore, is equitable and efficient from both an employer and an employee standpoint.

Insurance protection purchased by an employer is also more valuable to employees than equal cash compensation. This is because the premiums and, to a large extent, the benefits from group insurance aren't considered employee income, and thus aren't taxable as such. Life insurance premiums for protection in excess of $50,000 per year and disability benefits paid for by an employer are subject to income tax; some disability benefits are also subject to FICA tax. The vast majority of these premiums and benefits, however, as well as those associated with medical expense reimbursement, are tax-exempt.

-15-

What is a group insurance contract?

A group insurance contract is an agreement between an insurer and a policyholder. The insurer issues a master contract to the group policyholder to insure a group of individuals who have a common, defined relationship to that entity (employer, union, employer trust, association, etc.). The contract states the benefits, rights, and obligations of the parties. It is a promise by the insurance carrier to pay the benefits described for covered losses incurred by the insured individuals. In return, the policyholder promises to pay periodic premiums; the individuals are not parties to the contract and receive certificates of insurance as evidence of their coverage.

-16-

What types of group protection are available to employers?

Although there are many variations of each, the four major types of insurance coverage provided by employers to their employees are: life, accidental death and dismemberment (AD&D), disability, and health. Some employers also provide additional coverages, including group legal, travel accident, and vision and dental care.

-17-

What are the characteristics of group life insurance?

Group life insurance provides cash benefits to the insured employee's beneficiary in the event of the employee's death from any cause while covered under the group policy. The beneficiary is the insured's designated survivor or survivors. Although group life insurance can take many forms, the most common is term insurance. It has no cash value and will pay the face amount upon death of the employee. Some plans provide dependent life insurance, which pays the employee the face amount in the event of the death of a covered dependent.

-18-

What are the characteristics of group AD&D insurance?

AD&D insurance provides coverage for death or dismemberment

that results directly from accidental causes within, generally, 90 days of the injury. A lump-sum cash benefit is paid to the designated survivor of an insured who dies of accidental causes. The insured receives a smaller lump-sum cash benefit in the event of the accidental loss of a limb or eyesight.

-19-

How does group disability insurance protect against loss of income?

Group disability insurance provides cash payments to the insured for loss of a portion of income during a period of disability. The cash payments are often a percentage of the individual's weekly or monthly salary, or a fixed amount that does not exceed 70% of the individual's salary. Both short-term and long-term disability coverages are available. Short-term disability plans require a short period of disability before benefits begin; in the case of accidents, there is sometimes no time requirement before benefits begin. Long-term plans require total disability for much longer periods of time. Short-term disability coverage may replace earnings for 13 weeks, while long-term disability provides coverage until retirement or age 70. (It is considered likely that by 1987 even the age 70 cutoff will be removed by legislative action.)

-20-

What are the characteristics of group health insurance?

Group health insurance is sometimes used as a comprehensive term that includes medical, dental, disability, and AD&D insurance. In this text, group health insurance refers solely to medical insurance.

Group health insurance provides full or partial reimbursement for various medical expenses incurred by insureds. Coverage almost always includes reimbursement for hospital and surgical expenses and for diagnostic X-rays, tests, and physicians' visits. The full extent of coverage depends on the master contract issued to the group.

-21-

Why was group health insurance developed?

Group health insurance was originally developed to provide persons with financial protection from the expenses related to hospital confinement. The 1911 National Health Insurance Act of Great Britain made the United States aware of the concept of providing medical benefits to a group. In the following decade, several U.S. hospitals offered hospital expense benefits on an individual prepaid basis. Baylor University Hospital in Texas offered school teachers, who were members of a mutual benefit society, 21 days of hospital expense protection in any one year, with premiums paid in advance. The concept is considered the forerunner of Blue Cross plans.

The Depression awakened the public to the need for protection against medical expenses. It also helped spread Baylor Hospital's concept of group prepayment to other hospitals that were faced with declining revenues. In 1934, The Equitable Life Assurance Society of the United States provided General Tire and Rubber Company with group hospital expense insurance and soon Occidental Life of California offered similar coverage to other employers.

As more insurance companies began to offer hospital coverage, health coverage expanded to include reimbursement for surgical and doctors' expenses. Over the years, coverage for medical expenses has continued to grow to include reimbursement for such things as physical therapy, prescription drugs, and home health care.

-22-

What caused the rapid growth of group health insurance?

A number of factors contributed to the rapid growth of group health insurance. Among the more important factors are:

- Industrialization and urbanization, which caused changes in the values of an increasingly affluent society, and lessened the family's responsibility for the health care of infirm family members; and
- Wage controls during World War II, which caused employers to use rich employee benefits plans to attract employees during a period of short labor supply.

Labor was in the driver's seat, and unions demanded more and more benefits; favorable federal tax treatment made benefits a cost-effective way to increase employees' compensation with higher value to them than cash. The rising demand for, and cost of, medical care made health insurance a necessity. Social legislation, together with refinements in the group insurance concept, led to more and different groups being covered, and new benefits being added.

-23-

How important is group health insurance to employees?

Group health insurance, like group life or group disability insurance, has enabled employers to meet—at least in part—whatever responsibility they have to help employees and their dependents protect themselves against financial disaster from serious illness or injury. For many employees, participation in a group health plan at work is their only means of acquiring health insurance coverage. Group health insurance has made it possible for hundreds of millions of Americans, who for various reasons (inadequate income, uninsurability, etc.) would otherwise not be covered, to receive financial protection for major illness or injury.

-24-

How has group health insurance changed in recent years?

The most significant change in group health insurance in recent years is the expansion of coverage for medical expenses. Medical expense coverage now often includes some degree of reimbursement for preventive care, vision care, hospice care, confinement in a reputable nursing facility, outpatient treatment, and services of previously excluded practitioners such as midwives and chiropractors.

Another change has been the rapid escalation of health care costs. Americans place a high value on health care. This country spends millions of dollars annually on research and development related to disease treatment and prevention. However, the great strides made in technological and medical advances have not come cheaply. This cost is one of many factors reflected in the high price we pay for medical treatment today. Rising health care costs, in turn, have pushed up the cost of health insurance. As a result, we have seen much greater emphasis in recent years on designing benefits plans with cost-containment and cost-management features.

-25-

How much have health care costs increased in recent years?

In recent years, increases in medical costs have exceeded the increases in the consumer price index (see the Appendix). In addition, total health care spending (which includes both public and private expenditures for personal health care, medical research, construction of medical facilities, administrative and health insurance costs, and government-sponsored public health activities) has increased at double-digit rates for several years, and now accounts for over 10% of the gross national product.

Even though increases in health care costs remain higher than increases in the consumer price index, these costs are not rising as rapidly as before. This is due to a lower overall inflation rate and because of the cost-management efforts being developed by employers, insurers, the government, and health care providers.

Choosing an Intermediary

Because of limited resources and a lack of expertise, most small employers use an insurance professional—either an agent, broker, or consultant—to assist in the design, purchase, and administration of a group health insurance plan. This chapter examines the various types of professionals and the services they offer.

-26-

Can an employer work directly with an insurance company?

The majority of employers do not work directly with insurance companies. The rare exception is the very large company that has sufficient internal employee benefits expertise to do so.

Smaller employers particularly need a qualified professional because they lack the resources and expertise to handle their group insurance needs. An intermediary can help them define their needs and objectives, design a plan to meet those criteria, select the proper purchase and funding vehicles, obtain competitive quotes from insurers, and service the plan.

-27-

What is an intermediary?

An intermediary is a knowledgeable benefits professional who helps employers and other groups to develop, design, purchase, and service benefits plans. An intermediary may be a broker, an agent, an employee benefits consultant, or a third-party administrator (TPA).

-28-

What services do intermediaries provide prior to the purchase of a group health insurance plan?

The services that intermediaries provide will depend to a great extent on (1) the employer's own employee benefits expertise and (2) the type of intermediary the employer chooses. For employers with little or no knowledge of health insurance, the intermediary can provide all the elements of the plan, including designing it, determining how it should be funded, selecting an insurance carrier, and servicing the plan. Those employers that possess greater knowledge and resources, however, will likely play a more active role in the decision-making process. The type of intermediary the employer selects will also determine the extent of services provided.

-29-

What is an insurance broker?

An insurance broker is a representative of an employer who provides counsel on insurance-related issues and assistance in dealing with insurance companies. Brokers sell a variety of products and services, including business and group insurance, and market the products of many insurance companies.

Brokerage firms vary from the single broker operating independently to brokerage houses that employ thousands of professionals and operate offices nationally and internationally. They usually work with companies of over 100 employees, although some of the larger national houses have departments specifically set up to work with smaller employers.

-30-

What is the difference between an agent and a broker?

The basic difference between an agent and a broker is that while the broker represents the employer, the agent is generally under contract with an insurance company to sell all of its products. That is, agents represent sellers (insurance companies) and brokers represent buyers (employers).

If an agent's own company cannot meet the client's need, the agent will deal with another insurance company; in this case, the distinction between an agent and a broker becomes blurred. Agents work primarily with the smaller single-employer groups.

-31-

What is an employee benefits consultant?

Employee benefits consultants specialize in the analysis and design of an employer's entire noncash compensation program. They have greater depth of knowledge of a particular client's company, having often been hired to analyze that company's compensation objectives in detail. Their expertise may be especially useful to larger employers that elect to partially or totally self-fund their employee benefits plans. Also, some consultants, like certain brokers, act as administrators in providing continuing service to their clients. Some employers believe a consultant offers a more objective viewpoint, since consultants are compensated directly by the employer, usually on a fee-for-service basis.

-32-

How does an employer determine whether to use an agent, broker, or consultant?

Agents, brokers, and consultants provide many of the same services, and distinguishing among them is sometimes difficult. Generally, agents work with smaller companies (fewer than 100 employees) that are less likely to require extensive analysis of their compensation strategies. Some brokers, especially those associated with large national brokerage houses, provide some of the same services as consultants.

-33-

How does an employer select a particular intermediary?

Most small employers select an intermediary just as they would hire any outside professional help. They consult friends, business associates, and authorities they respect. Based on this information, the employer can develop a list of potential candidates. It is generally advisable to speak with several candidates, because it is important that an employer trust the intermediary and feel comfortable doing business with that person.

-34-

Can an employer use a personal or business advisor as its group insurance intermediary?

Yes. The employer can use the broker or agent who handles the employer's business or personal insurance as an advisor, if it is felt that this intermediary has the required degree of employee benefits expertise.

-35-

Why would an employer change intermediaries?

An employer would change intermediaries only if the expertise or services provided are not satisfactory.

-36-

How are intermediaries compensated?

Agents and brokers typically receive a percentage of premiums—commissions—from the insurance companies with whom they place business. Consultants generally charge either a fixed fee or an hourly rate to the employers for which they are providing services. In recent years, there has been a trend, especially among large brokerage houses, to negotiate a fee for services rendered. In addition, some individuals and firms will operate in either mode—commissions or fee-for-service.

-37-

What are commission schedules?

Commission schedules are a type of monetary incentive that insurance companies use to encourage agents and brokers to do business with their companies. The two most common types of commission schedules are the high-low schedule and the level commission schedule. Both reward agents and brokers by providing a percentage of the premium for the insurance that is sold.

The high-low commission schedule encourages group brokers and agents to place new business with a particular carrier by providing commissions that are a higher percentage of premiums the first year of coverage and a lower percentage in renewal years.

The level commission schedule provides the same percentage of premium each year, assuming the premium is the same each year. This type of schedule encourages a group producer to keep business with a carrier, since there is no decrease in commissions after the first year. Over time, the two types of schedules provide similar compensation. The following table compares them:

Commission Scale

	High-Low Schedule		*Level Schedule*
Annual Premium	*Year 1*	*Year 2–10*	*First 10 Years*
First $1,000	25.0%	6.5%	7.5%
Next $8,000	20.0%	3.0%	5.0%
Next $5,000	15.0%	2.0%	3.5%
Next $10,000	10.0%	2.0%	3.2%
Next $10,000	7.5%	2.0%	2.8%
Next $25,000	5.0%	1.5%	2.0%
Next $100,000	2.5%	1.0%	1.5%

-38-

What is vesting of commissions?

Vesting of commissions occurs when the insurer grants ownership of renewal commissions (commissions paid when coverage is renewed for another plan year) to the agent whether or not the agent renews with the insurer. Although insurers differ in their vesting procedures, there is a general trend away from this concept.

-39-

Are there laws that regulate the business practices of intermediaries?

State laws determining agent and broker licensing requirements vary from state to state and can require consultants to be licensed. Insurance companies monitor the licensure status of intermediaries that place business with them. Some states allow agents and brokers to operate in the state if they are licensed in another state.

-40-

What is a third-party administrator (TPA)?

TPAs are persons or organizations that are hired to provide certain administrative services to group benefits plans. Their functions may include premium accounting, claims review and payment, claims utilization review, maintenance of employee eligibility records, and negotiations with insurers that provide stop-loss protection for large claims. Sometimes a TPA also fills the role of the consultant-broker, in which case the TPA would help design the benefits plan and recommend the appropriate purchase and funding vehicles. However, TPAs are most commonly employed by association groups, trusts, and employers that self-fund. At the start of their business arrangement, the employer and TPA sign an agreement that outlines the services and authority of the TPA. If the employer's plan is only partially self-insured, most insurance companies reserve the right to approve the employer's TPA appointment.

-41-

If an employer wants to self-fund the plan, which type of insurance professional would it need?

An employer interested in partially or fully self-insuring its group insurance plan often works with an employee benefits consultant or a TPA. However, many agents and brokers will have the expertise necessary to design and properly structure the funding of the plan. If the compensation is suitably arranged, brokers or agents often administer plans for employers that self-fund their plans, or the insurance company may administer the plan even though it is not underwriting the entire risk.

-42-

Would an employer whose plan is fully insured use a TPA?

An employer with a fully insured plan may employ a TPA to handle the administrative functions of the plan. However, insurance companies provide most fully insured employers with administrative services.

-43-

How does an employer decide whether to use a TPA or an insurance company to administer its plan?

Both insurance carriers and TPAs provide valuable administrative services, which an employer would find difficult to provide internally. The choice between a TPA and an insurer should be based on service, ease of administration, and cost.

The employer should determine what services are most important. Some employers believe that local claims service is advantageous. The two traditional components of claims service are claims turnaround time and resolution of problems associated with claims. These services are not necessarily handled any more expediently with local service. Some employers may prefer a single source for all their insurance dealings.

In addition to accurate claims payment, an important service TPAs and insurance companies provide is giving the policyholder accurate information on benefits utilization. Examples of data reports should be requested from prospective administrators and compared. This is especially true for employers that have enough employees to be charged based on their own claims utilization.

-44-

If an employer has a partially or fully insured plan and has a TPA handle the administrative functions, would the employer's cost be decreased?

The employer's insurance premium would be decreased, since it eliminates the cost of administrative services provided by the insurance company. However, the employer would be paying the TPA for the services. Depending on what those services are, their cost, and the efficiency of the TPA, the employer's overall cost could be higher or lower.

-45-

How are TPAs compensated?

Most TPAs charge for their consulting services on either a fixed-fee or an hourly basis. All sorts of arrangements are made for administrative charges, but most TPAs charge for administrative services on a fixed-fee basis either monthly or per employee, in addition to a fixed rate applied to the number of benefits checks mailed to employees. The employer generally compensates the TPA directly.

-46-

What is a group sales representative?

A group sales representative is an employee of an insurance company who sells group insurance and performs a variety of functions in conjunction with consultants, agents, brokers, and, for some insurers, TPAs. The sales representative supplements the group insurance knowledge of the intermediary, especially with respect to the insurance company's products. Group sales representatives are often located in branch offices. They are compensated by their employers (insurance carriers) for placing business and servicing it.

-47-

How do group sales representatives and intermediaries interact in the sale of a group health insurance plan?

Group sales representatives of different insurance carriers approach intermediaries to explain their insurance products. In turn, intermediaries request quotes for plans to meet the needs of their clients. They may work together to determine the most appropriate plans and to discuss the premiums required for those plans.

-48-

What information would the intermediary provide to the group sales representative to solicit quotes?

Most insurance companies require at least a census listing of the employees to be covered under the prospective plan, the benefits plan design and alternatives, the funding vehicle, and the effective date of the plan. Once selected, the broker, agent, and group sales representative install the benefits plan, service the group, and present renewals to the employer. Intermediaries have also recently worked with carriers and clients on cost-containment activities.

-49-

What is the role of the intermediary in the ongoing maintenance of the plan?

The intermediary's role in the ongoing maintenance of the plan varies according to the particular intermediary and the services that were negotiated. For example, a TPA would generally handle plan administration. Some intermediaries stay closely involved and help make sure that employees are satisfied. They may handle all dealings with the insurance company.

-50-

What is a client service representative?

Some insurance companies have specialized personnel in their field offices that are trained to deal with intermediaries and clients in the ongoing administration of the health insurance plan. This enables the insurer to deal with clients' questions locally and to visit clients if necessary. Such specialized personnel are known as client service representatives.

Factors Influencing the Design of Group Health Insurance Plans

A variety of federal and state laws regulate the group health insurance market. These governmental factors, as well as important social and financial considerations, will strongly influence an employer's decision-making process. This chapter covers both the external and internal factors that affect the basic decisions concerning an employer's group health insurance plan. These statutes include state and federal laws like Medicare, ADEA, and ERISA, as well as requirements concerning size, eligibility, and participation in group health insurance plans.

-51-

Are employers legally required to purchase group insurance for their employees?

No federal law requires employers to provide their employees with group insurance. A few states do have laws that mandate short-term disability coverage for all employees. These states are New York, Rhode Island, California, New Jersey, and Hawaii; Puerto Rico also requires such coverage. If an employer does elect to provide employees with other group insurance benefits, there are both federal and state laws with which the plan must comply.

-52-

Are group health plans governed by federal or state laws?

Generally, insurance is governed by state, rather than federal, law. This was provided for by the McCarran-Ferguson Act, which, as of 1948, provided that federal law will regulate insurance only when state law does not. Each state has its own laws governing contracts, including those for insurance; and most states have laws specifically covering group life and health insurance.

States usually have an appointed official who oversees the operations of insurers in that state, commonly either a Superintendent or Commissioner of Insurance (see the "List of State Insurance Commissioners" section). In addition, the National Association of Insurance Commissioners, a voluntary organization of state insurance officials with influence but no legislative authority, has developed standard model bills and procedures that are designed to provide some consistency from state to state. Though consistency is growing on a state-to-state basis, when you begin to conduct business in a new state, it is advisable to contact your state insurance commissioner.

-53-

What are the responsibilities of the state insurance department?

The insurance department is the administrative agency that supervises the insurance companies doing business in that state. The insurance department is assigned the task of making sure that carriers obey the insurance laws. Areas of responsibility include: licensing of companies and agents, issuing regulations, conducting examinations of companies, making legislative recommendations, monitoring fares and rates, handling customer complaints, and developing model bills, and any other duty that will insure that state insurance laws are kept up-to-date and adequately enforced.

-54-

What are the similarities among state laws governing group health insurance?

Most states have very similar programs that govern each of the following: minimum participation, eligibility, certificates to insureds, payment of premiums, grace periods, claims processing, the appeals process, and the coordination of health insurance benefits among insureds' plans. Despite these somewhat standard provisions, laws governing specific benefits vary considerably from state to state. These state programs generally fall into two categories: mandated benefits and mandated offerings of benefits.

-55-

What is a mandated benefit?

A mandated benefit is a specific coverage that an insurer is required to include in its contract. For example, most states require that coverage for substance-abuse treatment be provided. Other kinds of coverage that are mandated in some states include coverage for newborn children, mental and nervous disorders, and hospice care.

Most states differ in the way they require the insurer to provide the mandated benefits. Some states require that benefits be provided on the same basis as for any other illness; others require that an insurer provide an annual maximum dollar amount or number of visits for each individual for claims relating to certain mandated benefits.

-56-

Why are some benefits mandated?

Some states mandate benefits because it is felt that there is a need that is not being covered satisfactorily. Benefits that are mandated are usually for a widely recognized social goal.

-57-

What is a mandated offering?

This provision is similar to the mandated benefit regulation. Whereas a mandated benefit is a *required* and integral aspect of the policy, a mandated offering is required only to be *offered* through certain coverages to each policyholder. The coverage is available at an additional price to the employer, and the employer is not required to purchase it. Unlike mandated coverage, it is not required to be a part of every insurance contract.

-58-

What are the state requirements for employee participation in a group insurance plan?

State laws require that insurance companies set participation percentages to ensure against adverse selection, which could jeopardize the insurer's solvency. In most states, the participation requirement is 75%. This means that at least 75% of an employer's eligible employees must participate in a group health insurance plan.

-59-

Who is an eligible employee?

An eligible employee is any employee designated by the employer to be covered under the plan. Employers vary widely on the definition of eligible employees.

-60-

What is the minimum number of employees allowed by state law to participate in a group health insurance plan?

Most states require that an employer enroll a minimum of 10 employees for coverage in order to purchase and maintain a group health insurance plan. This minimum size requirement reduces the potential for adverse selection. Employers with fewer than 10 enrolled employees often participate in a group trust, such as a multiple employer trust (MET).

-61-

Is there a maximum number of employees that may be covered under a group health insurance plan?

There is no legal limit to the number of employees that may be covered under a group health insurance plan. In fact, some plans cover tens of thousands of employees.

-62-

Can an employer legally choose which employees it wants covered under a group health insurance plan?

An employer may choose to cover only certain employees under a group health insurance plan, as long as the applicable employment laws are not violated. Federal laws that prohibit discrimination on the basis of age, sex, or race apply to an employer's health plan. Those criteria cannot be used as the basis for exclusion.

-63-

For what reasons do employers typically exclude employees from group health insurance coverage?

There are several reasons for excluding employees from coverage. For example:

- Union employees who have coverage that was negotiated as part of a collective bargaining agreement would be excluded.
- An employer may choose to cover employees working in different locations under different plans.
- A subsidiary of an employer may be in a different industry, and that industry may have different benefits needs; hence, the subsidiary could be excluded and covered under a different plan.
- An employer may want to give extra benefits to a special class of higher-paid employees and would, therefore, exclude all other employees from the extra coverage.
- The expense of covering part-time and temporary employees may be too great for the employer to consider covering them.

-64-

What federal laws affect group health insurance plans?

There are two general types of federal law that have a material impact on group health insurance plans. The first type involves those laws enacted primarily to protect employees from discrimination in employment. Although these laws do not specifically address group health insurance issues, they do contain relevant regulations. The most important of these laws are the Age Discrimination in Employment Act of 1967, as amended in 1978 (ADEA); the Employee Retirement Income Security Act of 1974 (ERISA); and Title VII of the Civil Rights Act of 1964, as amended.

The second type of federal law addresses specific health insurance issues. The most important of these include the 1965 amendment to the Old Age, Survivors' and Disability Insurance Act (OASDI), which established Medicare, effective July 1966; and the HMO Act of 1973. Two more recent laws, the Tax Equity and Fiscal Responsibility Act of 1982 (TEFRA) and the Deficit Reduction Act of 1984 (DEFRA), also affect the design of group insurance plans.

-65-

How does ADEA affect group health insurance plans?

ADEA prohibits discrimination in employment against individuals aged 40 to 70 (until 1983, the maximum age was 65). While the main intent of this law is to prohibit mandatory retirement before age 70 (with certain exceptions), related provisions of the law apply to health insurance. ADEA, as amended by TEFRA in 1982, requires employers with 200 or more employees to offer older active employees under age 70 who are eligible for Medicare (and their spouses if they are also under age 70) the same health insurance coverage that is provided to younger employees.

-66-

What other legislation affects group health benefits for employees eligible for Medicare?

For employers of 20 or more employees, TEFRA amended the Social Security Act to make Medicare secondary to employer group health plans for active employees and their spouses, aged 65 through 69. TEFRA also amended ADEA to require employers to offer employees aged 65 through 69 and their dependents the same coverage available to younger employees. Employers do have the right to reduce or terminate medical coverage for employees who are aged 70 or older. DEFRA further extended the law to require that group health plans be offered to dependents in the 65–69 age bracket, even if the employee is not in that age bracket.

Employees have the right to reject their employer's plan and elect only Medicare coverage. Employees can also choose to participate only in their employer's plan, even though they are eligible for Medicare. Or they can choose to have their Medicare benefits supplemented with benefits from their employer's group health insurance plan. In this case, the employer's plan would have to be coordinated with Medicare benefits to ensure that the employee receives no duplication of benefits. If the employer does provide coverage as a supplement to Medicare, the plan design may be written in one of three ways:

(1) Benefits payable under the employer's plan are reduced by the benefits payable under Medicare. Generally, the employer's plan covers the same benefits as Medicare but is reduced by the Medicare payments. This is commonly referred to as "carve out."

(2) Benefits payable under the employer's plan are specially designed to pay for expenses that Medicare does not cover.

(3) Benefits payable under the employer's plan are combined with Medicare benefits using a coordination of benefits provision, which allows the insured to be reimbursed for up to 100% of expenses allowable under either plan.

-67-

Why would employees choose Medicare as the primary payer?

Employees who are eligible for Medicare benefits and who also participate in a contributory health insurance plan may find that Medicare is a less expensive source of health care benefits.

-68-

What does Medicare cover?

Medicare consists of a hospital benefits plan (Part A) and supplementary medical insurance (Part B). Part A covers individuals for expenses incurred at hospitals, extended care facilities, home health care agencies, and hospices. Part A is automatic at no fee to eligible individuals. "Eligible" refers to individuals who are eligible for Social Security benefits (who are over age 65), or who are under age 65 and are eligible for Social Security because they receive Social Security disability income or receive treatment for end-stage kidney diseases. Individuals over age 65 but not eligible for Social Security benefits may enroll in Part A by paying a premium.

Part B helps pay for physicians' services and other medical services not paid for under Part A. Participation in Part B is voluntary and requires premium contributions by the individual to Medicare.

-69-

Are employers required by law to cover retired employees under group health insurance plans?

No. Employment law generally affects active employees. The decision to cover retirees is a human resource issue, rather than a legal requirement. The employer should examine its employee benefits objectives to decide whether or not to cover retirees. Many companies are encouraging early retirement to manage expenses and avoid layoffs; for them, it might be in their best interests to provide health insurance coverage to retirees. Most retirees have access to health insurance through Medicare, so coverage through an employer's plan would be supplemental. The cost of retiree coverage is high in spite of the share paid by Medicare. Recent court rulings have prohibited employers from changing existing retirees' promised coverage. Therefore, employers should evaluate the pros and cons carefully before implementing retiree coverage.

-70-

What requirements does ERISA impose on group health insurance plans?

ERISA was enacted primarily to effect pension equality, but it also protects the interests of group insurance plan participants and beneficiaries. Under ERISA, group health insurance plans must be established pursuant to a written instrument that describes the benefits provided under the plan, names the persons responsible for the operation of the plan, and spells out the arrangements for funding and amending the plan.

ERISA established a reporting procedure that requires that a summary plan description (SPD) be filed with the Department of Labor, and an annual financial report be filed with the Internal Revenue Service. However, most plans with fewer than 100 participants are not required to file these reports because Congress considered the reporting requirements too burdensome for small employers. Plan participants must be given copies of the SPD and the summary annual report (if the plan is subject to annual financial reporting).

-71-

Are employers required by law to provide employees with maternity benefits?

In 1978, an amendment was passed to the Civil Rights Act of 1964 that included legislation covering maternity benefits. Under this law, companies with 15 or more employees engaged in interstate commerce must provide the same benefits for pregnancy, childbirth, and related medical conditions that are provided for any other sickness or injury. Some states have their own maternity provisions in addition to those mandated by federal law; these provisions usually require employers to provide more maternity benefits, such as additional coverage during a complicated pregnancy. The Civil Rights Act of 1964, as amended in 1978, also mandates that an employer provide a dependent spouse of an employee covered under a plan the same maternity benefits as full-time employees. To date, maternity coverage for dependent daughters has not been mandated.

This law does not require coverage for abortions except when the life of the mother would be endangered if the fetus were carried to term or when medical complications have arisen from an abortion. An employer, however, may provide more liberal abortion benefits if it so desires, and most insurance carriers provide options regarding this coverage.

-72-

How are group health insurance plans affected by the HMO Act of 1973?

The provision of the HMO Act that has the most significant effect on group health insurance plans is the "dual choice option." This provision requires that employers with 25 or more employees in a health maintenance organization (HMO) service area include HMO coverage as an alternative to the employer's regular health plan. The law requires that at least onc group practice and one individual practice HMO be offered to employees if the employer receives a request for inclusion by each type. HMOs are responsible for requesting inclusion by employers as alternative health plans, and are subject to certain federal requirements in order for employers to be required to recognize them. Employers must make the same contribution on behalf of their employees to an HMO as they do for their other health care plans.

This dual choice option was established to encourage individuals to consider coverage under an HMO instead of under their employer's traditional plan. HMOs are discussed in detail in the chapter entitled "Alternative Health Care Systems."

-73-

What penalties are employers subject to if they fail to comply with the legal requirements governing group health insurance plans?

The penalties for employers that fail to comply with a regulation depend on the specific regulation. Insurance companies take responsibility for making sure their plans comply with the various state requirements regarding benefits. Failure to comply with laws regarding employment discrimination is a violation of federal (and possibly state) law.

-74-

What state tax laws apply to group health insurance plans?

All states tax the premiums that group insurance policyholders pay to insurers based on the residence of covered employees. These taxes range from 1% to 3.3% of premiums. The cost of the tax to insurance companies is passed along to the policyholder.

-75-

What is the federal tax status of group health insurance in relation to employers?

Under the Internal Revenue Code, an employer's contributions to a group health insurance plan are deductible as ordinary and necessary business expenses. There is no limit as to the amount that can be deducted, as long as the contributions qualify as additional reasonable compensation to the insured and the benefits are payable to the employees, not the employer.

An exception to this general rule concerns group insurance plans funded through voluntary employees' beneficiary associations (VEBAs), also known as 501(c)(9) trusts. VEBAs, which are minimally used by large employers, are subject to certain nondiscrimination requirements that must be met to qualify for preferred tax status.

-76-

Are employer contributions treated as taxable income to employees?

No. Contributions by an employer to a health insurance plan are not now considered part of an employee's taxable income. An exception to this involves amounts paid to highly compensated individuals covered under a discriminatory, self-insured medical expense reimbursement plan. In such plans, the contributions may be treated as taxable income. Legislative proposals have considered including part of the premiums for health insurance plans in the taxable income of employees. No such change has been made as of the publication of this book.

-77-

Do federal and state laws apply to self-insured group health plans?

Most federal laws that govern group health insurance plans also apply to self-insured plans, since they deal with employment practices rather than insurance. ERISA supersedes any state laws governing self-insured plans. However, the intent of ERISA continues to be challenged in the courts, and this information should be reaffirmed periodically.

-78-

When state and federal laws change, what are an employer's obligations regarding a group health insurance plan?

Insurers are required by law to write legally acceptable benefits plans and, therefore, take the responsibility for helping employers comply with the laws. Insurers generally take responsibility for informing employers about legislative developments. The insurer, with the intermediary, will explain exactly how the new law affects the employer and will outline how the employer's plan must change to comply with the new law. Sometimes the insurer will work with intermediaries to educate the employer.

Groups that self-fund must comply with laws that affect self-funded plans. Generally, the intermediary, TPA, or insurance company, if it is administering the plan, will take responsibility for informing the employer about legislative developments.

Changes to laws that affect group health insurance plans usually fall into one of three categories: laws that affect only policies issued after the effective date of the law; laws that not only affect newly issued policies but also require compliance at the next renewal date of an already existing policy; and laws that require compliance at any upcoming change to an existing policy, but at least at the next anniversary date of the policy. Some laws simply require that policyholders be offered the opportunity to purchase a new benefit. In that situation, the employer has the right to refuse to change the existing benefits plan.

-79-

Besides the legislative factors, what other issues must be addressed as part of the purchasing process?

To some extent, general economic conditions will determine what type of plan an employer can select. For example, if the economy is depressed or the outlook for the employer's industry is poor, the employer may not be in a position to offer a generous benefits plan. However, the employer must simultaneously determine what role the group health insurance plan will play in its hiring strategy. Should the employer set up a "rich" plan in order to gain a recruiting advantage over competitors by providing employees and prospective employees with a more attractive benefits package, or will it settle for a less competitive plan?

Company demographics will also be a factor. If the majority of a company's employees are young and, therefore, would value certain types of benefits more than a predominantly older employee population would, the benefits plan can be structured to meet those needs. In addition, the employer will have to determine how its corporate culture should be manifested in the plan (e.g., a traditionally employee-oriented company will want a benefits plan that reflects that orientation). Some employees may already have insurance from other sources.

-80-

Can a single group health insurance plan meet the benefits needs of an employer's diverse work force?

Most group health insurance plans are comprehensive enough to cover a wide range of medical expenses. They provide coverage to protect even those in the employer's work force with the greatest need for health insurance. Ironically, the comprehensive nature of today's group benefits plans has created two new problems: duplication of benefits, and coverage levels not needed by many of today's workers. Because today's work force contains a growing number of two-wage-earner families—with both earners entitled to health coverage from their own employers—the potential for duplication of benefits is great.

-81-

Why would an employer offer benefits to which some employees already have access?

Health coverage has become an expected part of an employer's total compensation package, and if an employer hopes to attract and retain quality employees, medical coverage is among the first types of noncash compensation the employer should consider. A group plan allows all employees to participate without evidence of insurability. This is a valuable commodity to employees and their dependents who have health problems and are unable to purchase individual protection.

Although most employees have access to coverage (e.g., individual insurance, HMO, etc.), many do not elect it, usually due to the cost. Other employees may have "known" health conditions that either prevent them from obtaining individual coverage altogether or make the cost of that coverage so expensive that they can't afford it. Employees who receive coverage from a spouse's plan are dependent on the continued employment of that spouse for health insurance. In addition, receiving dependent coverage through a spouse is generally more expensive for the employee's family than for that employee to be covered in a group employee plan where he or she works.

-82-

Should an employer provide group health insurance to part-time and temporary employees?

Many employers do not cover part-time and temporary employees under their group health plans. Part-time employees are defined most often as those who work less than either 20 or 30 hours per week, depending on the industry. In general, employers believe that while these workers provide a valuable service, they do not justify the considerable expense associated with health benefits, particularly when they may be working for the company only a short time.

Some employers do choose to cover part-time and temporary employees, although it is often difficult to find a carrier that will include these workers in a group health insurance plan. Insurance companies believe these employees may be worse health risks than full-time permanent employees. However, due to changes in employment practices, such as job sharing among employees who choose to work part time while raising families, more coverage is being made available to part-time employees.

-83-

Why are part-time and temporary employees considered a worse risk?

Because part-time and temporary workers may have less need to work, they may have less motivation to recuperate and rehabilitate after an illness or injury. This can result in higher medical bills and, consequently, a higher cost of insurance. Also, the possibility of run-out obligations, which are medical expenses that an insurer is obligated to cover after the employee terminates employment, is increased because of the higher turnover and lack of stability of part-time and temporary employees. This, in turn, increases the risk to the insurer.

-84-

Can an employer provide enhanced health care coverage for key employees?

Under current tax law, different benefits can be provided to different classes of employees based on a condition of employment (e.g., salaried versus hourly employees). In addition, an employer can provide key employees with what is known as a medical reimbursement plan, which supplements the company's group health care plan. This arrangement typically reimburses employees for *any* medical expense not covered by the regular medical benefit plan. For example, a typical health plan does not cover eyeglasses; a medical reimbursement plan might reimburse an employee or dependent for this expense. (The tax law applicable to medical expense reimbursement defines "excess reimbursement," and should be reviewed by any employer contemplating the addition of a medical expense reimbursement plan.)

The employer can insure or self-insure this program. If the employer self-insures, reimbursements to "highly compensated" individuals will be taxable to those individuals if the employer discriminates in favor of them. If an employer is providing only key employees with this additional medical expense reimbursement plan, it is very likely that the employer is discriminating.

The Internal Revenue Code defines a "highly compensated individual" as one who falls into any *one* of the following classifications:

- An employee who is one of the five highest paid officers;
- A shareholder who owns more than 10% in value of the stock of the employer; or
- An employee who is among the highest paid 10% of all employees.

If an employer seeks to avoid having employees' reimbursements taxed as income, it may elect to *insure* the plan. Insured plans do not have to meet the nondiscrimination requirements for providing reimbursements to employees. (See IRC Section 105(h)(6).) But unless the policy involves the shifting of risk to an unrelated third party, the plan will be considered *self-insured.* Thus, a policy that provides only administrative or bookkeeping services will be considered self-insured.

-85-

Will an insurance carrier deny certain employees coverage under a group health insurance plan?

Generally, insurers won't deny coverage to any full-time employee. Inherent in the principle of group insurance is the understanding that all employees can be covered. Most carriers, however, require an employee to be actively at work on the day the employer's coverage becomes effective, and to have enrolled in a contributory plan within the time required.

Rather than deny certain employees insurance, most insurers reduce the chance of adverse selection by (1) requiring evidence of insurability if an employee wishes to enroll late or (2) placing restrictions on the coverage. The most common restriction is the preexisting-condition limitation. It is intended to limit payments on charges resulting directly from an accident or an illness for which the employee received medical treatment or care within a specified period of time prior to the date he or she becomes insured. The coverage may provide only a limited benefit for the preexisting condition, such as $1,000 for the first year the coverage is in effect. Some policies provide a more generous benefit; the amount the insurer will pay can range from no payment to as much as $10,000 in the first year. Some policies require a waiting period for coverage of a preexisting condition, which can vary in length from three months to two years. This preexisting-condition restriction usually is not applicable after the individual has been insured under the plan for 12 months.

Because employers use employee benefits to attract quality employees, it makes good business sense to cover new hires under the group health insurance plan from their first day on the job. Some employers provide immediate health benefits only for certain job grades or levels, specifically indicating those individuals for whom the employer uses benefits as a recruiting tool.

The other new hires are subject to a waiting period of between one and three months before their enrollment in the plan becomes effective. A waiting period is advantageous to companies that suffer from significant turnover because the administration involved in adding new employees to the plan and the risk associated with many short-term insureds is reduced considerably. Employees who are subject to a waiting period may purchase individual health policies to provide temporary insurance until they are eligible under the group health plan.

-86-

How much can an employer expect to pay annually for group health insurance?

The cost of group health insurance varies geographically and by plan, but in 1986, the estimated average annual cost per employee nationwide is approximately $780. The estimated cost for family (employee plus dependents) coverage is $2,184. A company in which 60% of the employees elected dependent coverage can expect to pay on average $1,622.40 per employee a year.

-87-

Must employers pay the entire cost of group health insurance?

No. Group health insurance plans can be noncontributory or contributory. Under a noncontributory plan, the employer pays the entire cost of the plan. Employees are automatically covered as soon as they become eligible for insurance coverage. Noncontributory plans have 100% participation.

Under a contributory plan, the employee shares in the cost of the plan. Once employees are eligible to participate in a contributory group health plan, they have 30 days in which to enroll. This is the enrollment period, and employees who elect coverage during this period do not have to submit medical evidence of insurability. If an employee does not elect coverage during the enrollment period, he or she may enroll at another time, but coverage will be subject to medical evidence of insurability. Enrollment periods are limited to specific times of the year, usually January 1 and July 1.

-88-

What factors should an employer consider when deciding if its group health insurance plan should be contributory or noncontributory?

The employer's decision will depend on how competitive the job marketplace is, what the competitors in the marketplace are doing, and the amount of money the employer can afford. Some employers want their employees to share in the cost of health coverage to make them aware of and responsive to its cost. The trend in health insurance is to place greater financial responsibility on the insureds for premiums and expenses, thereby helping to ensure that employees use the plan as efficiently as possible.

The following table illustrates how businesses typically distribute the cost of group health insurance:

	Employee Coverage	*Dependent Coverage*
Company A	100% noncontributory	100% noncontributory
Company B	100% noncontributory	50% contributory
Company C	10% contributory	50% contributory
Company D	25% contributory	25% contributory

-89-

What legal constraints are imposed on the distribution of employer-employee costs for group health insurance?

There are no legal requirements for employer-employee cost sharing.

-90-

How are costs distributed between employer and employee when benefits are union negotiated?

Unions traditionally negotiate noncontributory plans; however, this trend started to reverse as medical coverage became increasingly more costly.

-91-

Can an employer self-fund a group health insurance plan?

Yes. In fact, large companies with more than 500 employees often self-fund all or part of their group health insurance plans. The employer's objectives would be to improve cash flow, save premium taxes, eliminate the insurer's risk charge, and benefit from better than expected claims experience.

-92-

How common are self-funded plans?

Self-funded plans are more prevalent among larger employers.

They are not nearly as common for employers with under 250 employees.

-93-

What factors should a small employer consider when deciding whether to self-fund all or part of its health insurance plan?

A small employer must decide whether it can accept the total risk. If not, an insurer must be found to assume part of it, and the employer must decide whether possible savings are worth the added risk of highly fluctuating claims levels. If protection is purchased to eliminate that risk, the employer must determine its cost.

Depending on what technique is used, the employer must decide whether added administrative costs would wipe out any savings that might result from partial self-funding. There are alternative funding techniques, such as extended grace periods and retrospective premium payment arrangements, that provide some advantages at reasonable cost and risk.

Types of Health Insurance Plans and Benefits

With hundreds of insurance companies offering group health insurance plans, it is often difficult for smaller employers to determine exactly which plan will best meet their business objectives and their employees' health care needs. This chapter examines the different types of plans available and what benefits they provide.

-94-

What types of plans are available?

There are generally two types of group health insurance plans available to smaller employers: a basic medical plus major medical plan, commonly referred to as a "base plus" or "first dollar" plan, and a comprehensive medical plan, called simply "comprehensive." Because it is believed to be more cost-effective, the trend in plan design is clearly toward the comprehensive plan.

-95-

What is a base plus plan?

A base plus plan is a two-part health insurance plan. Basic medical coverage—for such expenses as hospital, surgical, physicians' visits, and diagnostic laboratory tests and X-rays—is provided under the first part. There may be limits on these expenses, such as a limited number of hospital days and a surgical schedule, but no deductible or coinsurance applies to the covered expenses. The employee is reimbursed starting with the first dollar of expenses.

The second, or major medical, part of the plan covers more "catastrophic" health problems that are unpredictable and difficult to budget for. The coverage is broad and substantial, with fewer limits. While these expenses are also paid for by the plan, a deductible is required before the employee is reimbursed for expenses. The coinsurance is applied until the maximum employee out-of-pocket expense is reached. Further covered expenses are reimbursed in full. (See the chart at Question 96.)

This two-part plan is the result of the historical development of health insurance. When first offered, group health insurance extended only basic medical coverage. This was followed years later by broader coverage for more catastrophic illness.

-96-

What is a comprehensive plan?

A comprehensive plan provides coverage for most medical services using one reimbursement formula. In a pure comprehensive plan, a deductible must be met before reimbursement for any covered expenses begins, and coinsurance applies to all covered expenses until the maximum employee out-of-pocket expense limit is reached. Additional covered expenses are paid in full. There have been many modifications to the pure comprehensive design to meet various market needs. For example, some employers have comprehensive plans with hospital expenses fully covered, with no deductible or coinsurance requirements. This form was first used by employers that wanted to move gradually away from a base plus plan.

The chart below shows the difference in design between base plus and comprehensive plans:

Base Plus Plan	
100% of balance to maximum	
80% Coinsurance	20%
Deductible	
Basic plan benefits (hospital, surgical, other medical, or Blue Cross/Blue Shield)	

Comprehensive Plan	
100% of balance to maximum	
80% Coinsurance	20%
Deductible	

-97-

Are there advantages to a base plus plan?

Base plus plans have been in existence longer than comprehensive plans; thus, many employers have had experience and feel comfortable working with them. From the employee's point of view, base plus plans appear to provide more generous benefits, because of the lack of deductibles and coinsurance in the basic medical part. Also, although it is generally not true, the major medical coverage gives employees the impression that they are receiving supplemental coverage that pays for everything the basic medical coverage does not.

-98-

What are the advantages of a comprehensive plan?

Because employees share from the beginning in the cost of their medical expenses when they are incurred, a comprehensive plan encourages them to use more cost-effective health care. For example, if an individual's physician recommends surgery and a hospital admission, the base plus plan would require no deductible or coinsurance to begin with. The patient who pays nothing for health care is less inclined to question the cost of it or to ask about alternatives. An individual covered by a comprehensive plan must satisfy a deductible and pay coinsurance before hospitalization expenses will be reimbursed. This patient is more likely to be cost-conscious and to seek out more cost-effective health care services and providers. Furthermore, the higher the deductible, the greater the influence on employees' utilization of medical services.

The cost-sharing feature of comprehensive plans makes them generally less expensive to employers, with price differentials ranging from 5% to 12%. In addition, one reimbursement formula is applied to all covered expenses.

-99-

Do all insurers offer both types of group health insurance plans?

Most private insurers offer both base plus and comprehensive plans, although recently some insurers have decided not to market base plus plans due to the greater simplicity and cost-control provided by comprehensive plans. Also, Blue Cross/Blue Shield (BC/BS) recently started offering a comprehensive plan as an alternative to its traditional base plus plan. However, while most insurers are similar in that they offer the two plan types and assume the insurance risks and the ongoing administration of the plans, the benefits provided by the plans and the specific plan features vary by insurer.

-100-

Are BC/BS plans similar to those offered by insurance companies?

BC/BS plans have traditionally been similar to private insurance company base plus plans. BC/BS usually offers both a base plus and a major medical plan, but some employers purchase only the base plus plan from "the Blues." This is because the Blue Cross base plan in some areas is less expensive than private insurance. The Blue Cross hospital discounts can be significant. An employer may elect a private insurer's major medical plan as a supplement, however, due to better price, coverage, or service.

-101-

Do most private insurers offer similar major medical supplements?

Generally, major medical plans offered by private insurance companies to supplement a Blue Cross base plan fall into two categories: supplemental major medical and wraparound major medical. The difference between the two is that the wraparound plan covers some basic expenses, such as surgery, and also covers major medical expenses, whereas the supplemental plan provides only major medical coverage. In the latter case, the surgical and doctors' charges would usually be covered by Blue Shield, which may or may not be operating jointly with Blue Cross.

Employers that like the Blue Cross hospital coverage but want a different plan for all their surgical coverage often elect wraparound plans.

-102-

How are BC/BS plans different from those offered by insurance companies?

BC/BS has different relationships with the providers of health care than do private health insurance companies. The Blues also use different reimbursement structures and determine premium rates on a different basis.

-103-

How does BC/BS differ from private insurers in its relationship with health care providers?

BC/BS contracts directly with physicians and hospitals to establish the level of charges it will pay for services rendered to its insureds. When an insured incurs a covered health care expense, the health care provider—a participating hospital or physician—bills BC/BS directly. Payment is made to the provider based on the already agreed-to payment schedule, which is accepted as payment in full.

This unique payment system between health care providers and the BC/BS network is an extension of the historically close relationship the Blues have maintained with the U.S. medical community over the years. This association dates back to the 1930s, when Blue Cross was established under the auspices of the American Hospital Association; Blue Shield was established by the American Medical Association in the 1940s. Blue Cross promised hospitals prompt payment and first-dollar reimbursement, thus guaranteeing that a patient's bill would be paid in full. In return, the hospitals gave Blue Cross a discount on hospital services for Blue Cross insureds. The ability to obtain large discounts from hospitals has given the Blues a significant competitive edge over private insurers, and in some areas of the country, BC/BS has gained a large share of the third-party reimbursement market.

-104-

Are expenses reimbursed at a more generous level by private insurers than by BC/BS?

Today, employers can choose from a variety of plans from BC/BS or private companies. Thus, it is the plan itself that dictates reimbursement, not the insurer. In the past, however, patients were sometimes better off with a Blue Cross plan because Blue Cross's full-payment charges were negotiated with health care providers. A private insurance plan would reimburse the insured for only a set amount in accordance with the plan limits, but a hospital's charges were sometimes above that. The hospital would then bill the individual for the balance.

> ***Example:*** Blue Cross has negotiated a room and board rate with Hospital X of $240 per day. If a Blue Cross insured is a patient at Hospital X, the hospital is obligated to accept $240 as full payment from Blue Cross. If the individual has private insurance for which there have been no provider-insurer charge negotiations, the same hospital might charge $290 per day. The original private hospital insurance plans reimbursed for fixed amounts, such as "$250 per day for 90 days per calendar year." If Hospital X billed the individual for $290, the plan would pay only $250, leaving the insured to pay the $40 balance. Today, private insurance company plans usually reimburse individuals for semiprivate room expenses, and there is no balance billing for the insured unless a private room is used.

-105-

How are BC/BS premium rates different from those of private insurers?

The negotiated hospital discounts arranged through BC/BS plans sometimes allow BC/BS to offer lower rates to employers. Also, BC/BS is a nonprofit organization in most states, and as such pays no premium tax to the state.

-106-

What other types of health care plans might an employer offer?

Some employers may offer a health maintenance organization (HMO) as an option in their group health insurance plans, and some of their employees may choose to participate. In addition, in recent years, medical care providers and medical care insurers have been working together to establish preferred provider organizations (PPOs) to build relationships similar to those that the Blues have with providers. HMOs and PPOs are explained in detail in the chapter entitled "Alternative Health Care Systems."

-107-

What is a deductible?

A deductible is a set dollar amount that an individual must pay (or "satisfy") before reimbursement for expenses begins. The primary purpose of the deductible is to encourage employees to utilize health care services only when necessary, and to discourage submission of small claims to the insurance company because of the administrative expense involved. Deductibles typically range from $50 to $1,000, or even higher. The higher the deductible, the lower the cost of the health insurance plan to the employer.

-108-

What is a carry-over deductible?

A carry-over deductible allows covered expenses incurred in the last three months of the prior calendar year to be carried over to the new year and counted toward satisfying the new year's deductible. This provision is included to avoid the financial hardship to an insured of having to pay a deductible in the last quarter of one year and another in January of the next year.

-109-

For insured employees with dependent coverage, does the deductible for each person have to be satisfied before reimbursement begins?

Each person covered under a group health insurance plan must meet a deductible before expenses will be covered. However, plans usually include some type of family deductible in order to limit a family's exposure to health care expenses.

The family deductible is set at some multiple of the individual deductible, generally two or three times. For the family deductible to be satisfied, the combined expenses of several family members are accumulated. Some plans require, however, that at least one family member satisfy the full individual deductible for the family deductible to be met.

-110-

What is coinsurance?

Coinsurance is a feature found in most group health insurance plans. It sets forth the percentage of covered expenses that the employees and the health insurance plan will pay. Under a base plus plan, no coinsurance is involved for basic medical coverage. For the major medical part of a base plus plan, and for a comprehensive plan, a coinsurance provision applies. The most common coinsurance level is one in which the employee pays 20% of the expenses, and the insurer pays 80%. This is called 80% coinsurance.

-111-

What is a maximum out-of-pocket expense?

A maximum out-of-pocket (OOP) expense is the maximum amount that an insured employee will have to pay for expenses covered under the plan. The most common OOP maximums are $500 and $1,000. Like the deductible, OOP maximums are increasing because greater cost sharing by employees is a tool for controlling benefits utilization. All expenses in excess of the OOP maximum are paid by the insurer without coinsurance. This is true even in cases in which an employee's coinsurance obligation would have exceeded the OOP maximum. For example, assume 80% coinsurance and a $1,000 OOP maximum. The employee (after satisfying the deductible) has a $20,000 bill for expenses covered under the plan. With 80% coinsurance, the employee apparently would have to pay $4,000 (20%), and the insurer $16,000 (80%). With a $1,000 OOP maximum, however, the employee's total expense would be limited to $1,000. Thus, a maximum OOP puts a cap on the cost of a catastrophic illness, at least for covered expenses under the plan.

-112-

Is the deductible included in determining an OOP maximum?

Some group health insurance plans do not include the deductible in their OOP limits. In such situations, the limit the insured employee would be responsible for paying would be the sum of the deductible and the OOP maximum. Other plans do include the deductible as part of the OOP maximum.

-113-

Can medical expenses not covered by a health insurance plan be applied toward the deductible or OOP maximum?

No. The expenses incurred by the insured employee must be covered expenses under the health insurance plan to be applied toward the deductible or OOP maximum.

-114-

What is a covered benefit or covered expense?

A covered benefit is a benefit provided for under a group health insurance plan. A covered expense is an expense incurred by an insured employee that will be reimbursed under the group health insurance plan. For example, with most health insurance plans, doctors' visits are a covered benefit. That is, a doctor's fee up to the amount provided by the plan will be reimbursed by the insurer.

-115-

Are all covered expenses reimbursed?

No. The fact that an expense or benefit is covered does not mean that the coverage is unlimited. Both base plus and comprehensive plans have limits to the expenses for which they will reimburse. In addition, as described above, both plans require some form of deductible and coinsurance.

-116-

Are covered expenses limited?

Insurers limit covered expenses in a variety of ways. One way is to cap allowable payments for a certain procedure or service. A common example of this type of limit would be a surgical schedule. Insurers also restrict covered expenses by limiting the number of visits or days for home health care or skilled nursing care, or by establishing a reasonable and customary charge.

-117-

What types of benefits are generally covered by a group health insurance plan?

Base plus and comprehensive plans vary by insurer, but generally cover the same kinds of benefits. These include:

- Professional services of doctors of medicine and osteopathy, and other recognized medical practitioners;
- Hospital charges for semiprivate room and board and other necessary services and supplies;

- Surgical charges;
- Services of registered nurses and, in some cases, licensed practical nurses;
- Home health care;
- Physiotherapy;
- Anesthetics and their administration;
- X-rays and other diagnostic laboratory procedures;
- X-ray or radium treatment;
- Oxygen and other gases and their administration;
- Blood transfusions, including the cost of blood when charged;
- Drugs and medicines requiring a prescription;
- Specified ambulance services;
- Rental of durable mechanical equipment required for therapeutic use;
- Artificial limbs and other prosthetic appliances, except replacement of such appliances;
- Casts, splints, trusses, braces, and crutches; and
- Rental of a wheelchair or hospital-type bed.

-118-

What is a reasonable and customary charge?

A reasonable and customary charge, also called a usual, reasonable, and customary charge, and referred to as an R&C, is the maximum amount that an insurer will reimburse for a medical care expense covered under the group health insurance plan. These amounts are usually determined from a database that identifies the cost of each procedure or service in various regions of the country. For example, to determine at what level to reimburse a surgeon's fee for a certain type of operation, an insurance company will examine the fees of all surgeons located within a certain geographic area. An R&C could be set so that some percentage, such as 90% of all surgeons' fees, would be covered. That is, if 1,000 surgeons' fees are reviewed, and 10% of the surgeons charge more than $5,000 and 90% charge less, the maximum covered charge would be $5,000 for that surgical procedure. That portion of the surgeon's charges over the R&C amount would not be considered a covered expense under the plan. R&C charges are adjusted periodically.

-119-

What is a schedule of insurance?

A schedule of insurance sets forth a specific maximum amount an insurer will pay for each procedure, such as surgery or radiotherapy procedures. Schedules are sometimes denominated in units, rather than in dollars. These are called relative value schedules; a factor that reflects the level of charges in a geographic area multiplied by the number of units provided for each procedure determines the maximum amount the plan will pay.

-120-

What kinds of hospital charges are covered under a group health insurance plan?

Group health insurance plans typically cover a variety of inpatient and outpatient charges. Inpatient covered charges include room, board, and necessary services and supplies.

Room and board charges are covered on a per-day basis up to either a maximum dollar amount each day or the most common semiprivate room and board charges of the particular hospital. Private rooms are generally not covered. *Base* plans cover hospital stays up to a certain number of days, such as 90 or 180 days per calendar year. The major medical plan covers days exceeding the base plan limit. Some base plans do cover 365 days of room and board, leaving major medical to cover only certain ancillary charges associated with the stay. *Comprehensive* plans typically cover *all* hospital days at the semiprivate room rate.

Hospital services and supplies include items such as drugs and use of the operating room. Some base plans allow maximum dollar amounts for these expenses; others cover them in full for the days covered for room and board. Comprehensive plans cover the same services the base plus major medical plans do, but a deductible and coinsurance are required from the start on comprehensive plans, as compared with base plans that pay for hospital stays at 100%, and major medical plans that pick up coverage when the base plan runs out. Of course, major medical requires a deductible and coinsurance.

Intensive care is usually covered up to two or three times the room and board allowances for a semiprivate room. Some plans cover intensive care at the R&C charge for the service.

-121-

What alternatives to hospital care are common today?

The most common alternative is the freestanding care center, also known as a "surgicenter" or "quick clinic." Some of these centers offer outpatient surgery under general anesthesia and some offer only routine, noninvasive care. Other alternatives are skilled nursing facilities. Patients discharged from acute care facilities find less expensive, more appropriate care at these extended care centers during their convalescence. See Question 128.

-122-

What kinds of hospital outpatient expenses are covered?

Three kinds of hospital outpatient care are covered: emergency treatment, surgery, and services rendered in the outpatient lab or X-ray department. Newer comprehensive plan design encourages the use of outpatient services (when appropriate) by covering them at a more generous level than hospitalization.

-123-

How is surgery covered under a health insurance plan?

Surgical expense benefits are provided on a scheduled or nonscheduled basis. Scheduled plans specify an allowance for each kind of surgery, either in dollar terms or relative to other procedures listed. Nonscheduled plans cover surgical expenses on a reasonable and customary basis. Basic plans have traditionally provided for surgery in conjunction with hospitalization. Today, base plus plans cover surgery wherever performed, to discourage unnecessary hospitalization. The plan benefits include payment for the surgeon, assistant surgeon, and anesthesiologist. Charges associated with the surgery, such as blood products, are also covered under the plan, although sometimes only up to a maximum amount, whereupon the major medical plan takes over.

Some employers purchase a plan that does not cover surgical charges. They purchase a wraparound major medical plan that covers surgery in addition to the standard major medical features. Comprehensive plans cover surgery after the insured satisfies a deductible. Coinsurance usually applies, but some plans encourage outpatient (as opposed to hospital) surgery by waiving the coinsurance provision in an effort to manage medical care costs.

-124-

Why do some plans pay R&C charges and others schedule benefits?

These differences are due in part to the evolution of health insurance benefits coverage. The earliest plans used schedules paying limited and controlled amounts for the procedures covered. As plans were expanded, R&C fees replaced schedule amounts (usually for surgery) to meet the market demand for full payment for expenses incurred. As charges increased, reimbursement automatically increased.

Some employers would like to return to schedules, because without them, their premiums increase significantly as physicians increase their R&C charges. This change would be difficult to implement. Employees would perceive it as a reduction in benefits, due to the more generous payment expectations today under the R&C system. This situation may change as more charges are based on DRGs.

-125-

If the physicians' charges exceed the R&C amount or the schedule amount, is the employee responsible for paying the balance?

Yes. An insured is responsible for any charge that exceeds the R&C or schedule amount.

-126-

How have hospital and surgical care changed recently?

The number of hospital procedures has decreased considerably, and patients who do enter hospitals for care are released more quickly. In addition, procedures once considered unsafe on an outpatient basis are now performed that way routinely. These changes have resulted from improved technology, increased competition in the health care market among different kinds of providers and facilities, and the growing concern about rising health care costs.

-127-

How are nonsurgical physicians' services covered?

Under a base plus plan, the basic medical part often covers physicians' fees to hospital patients up to a specified maximum, and for a duration that normally coincides with the duration of the hospital benefits. Base plans usually also provide for limited home or alternative care facility physicians' visits directly related to recuperation after a hospital discharge. In addition, "office" visits are usually covered, but are limited to a dollar amount per visit or per illness, or a maximum number of visits per calendar year. Major medical plans pick up the coverage for physicians' visits where the base plan coverage leaves off.

Comprehensive plans cover physicians' services in the hospital, at alternative care facilities, at home, or in the office. Deductibles and coinsurance apply.

Not all physicians' services are covered by group health insurance plans. For example, physicians' services for dental treatments or examinations and for the prescription or fitting of eyeglasses or hearing aids are commonly excluded.

-128-

Does health insurance cover extended care facilities?

Extended care facilities are of three types: skilled nursing care, intermediate care, and custodial care. Most health plans cover skilled care facilities for a maximum number of days per calendar year per patient, or specify a dollar amount per day that will be covered. Usually, a patient must have been hospitalized within 7 to 14 days before entering a skilled nursing facility in order to be eligible for benefits. Health insurance plans do not cover custodial nursing care and intermediate care may or may not be covered.

Base plans typically cover stays in skilled nursing facilities similarly to hospital expenses (i.e., a maximum benefit per day, to a maximum number of days in a calendar year). Major medical plans supplement this by providing additional days of care and by covering expenses associated with the care, all subject to deductible and coinsurance provisions until the maximum OOP is reached. Comprehensive plans usually pay for a set number of days of care, such as 28 per calendar year, subject to deductible and coinsurance provisions until the OOP maximum is reached, whereupon the plan would pay 100% of the reasonable and customary charges.

-129-

Are mental illnesses usually covered by health plans?

Group health insurance plans generally limit coverage for mental illnesses, because of a lack of understanding and agreement among health care professionals about the nature and causes of mental illnesses. It is difficult for insurers to make judgments, and thus calculate benefits payments and costs, without defined criteria for what is appropriate medical treatment, as they do for surgery, for example. Thus, they prevent excessive utilization of the mental illness benefit and limit their financial risk by limiting the coverage available in any given calendar year.

-130-

Is treatment for alcoholism and other types of substance abuse covered under typical health insurance plans?

Coverage for treatment of alcoholism and other forms of substance abuse is often limited under health plans. The limitations are similar to those for mental illnesses, and are imposed because appropriate treatment is difficult for health care professionals to define, thus making expected claims and an appropriate price for coverage difficult to establish. However, substance abuse is a growing problem for employers, and increased health care coverage would allow many employees to receive badly needed treatment.

-131-

Are all prescription drugs covered under health care plans?

Generally, only prescription drugs that are for treatment of an illness or injury are covered, subject to applicable deductibles and coinsurance. Many plans do not cover contraceptive prescription drugs, for example, or nicotine chewing gum prescribed for smokers trying to quit.

-132-

Will some plans cover contraceptive prescription drugs?

Yes. In fact, most prescription drug card plans offer plans "with or without contraceptives."

-133-

What is a prescription drug card plan?

Instead of reimbursing individuals for their drug purchases using the standard retrospective reimbursement process (involving claim forms), some employers elect a prescription service plan as part of their health plans. All covered individuals are issued prescription drug cards that allow them to "charge" their drug purchases. The plan sets a deductible amount that must be paid by the insured every time the card is used to purchase a prescription. Typically, this deductible is between $1 and $5. The pharmacy collects the deductible, completes the charge slip, and dispenses the drug. The pharmacy bills the prescription drug card company for the drug plus administrative expenses, and the prescription card company bills the insurance company (usually monthly) for the batch of prescriptions provided to its insureds.

-134-

Is a prescription drug card plan better than regular reimbursement?

Individuals like prescription drug cards because claim forms are eliminated and they often get more drug expenses covered. Health plans without prescription drug card programs require that the calendar-year deductible be satisfied before drug expenses are reimbursable. The majority of these individuals do not meet the deductible, and thus get no reimbursement for various antibiotics or analgesics routinely prescribed for minor illnesses or injuries. Further, for those who *do* meet the deductible, coinsurance still applies to drug expenses.

Insurers like drug card plans because the drug card administrators assume the administrative responsibilities of claims processing and control. Insurance companies without card programs process claims and cut reimbursement checks for individuals' drug expenses—an expensive process, due to the volume of claims. Prescription card administrators streamline the claims process through standardized forms and procedures and a network of participating pharmacies that follow these procedures and make batch claims processing possible. A few insurers have developed their own drug card administration to further control costs by eliminating the middleman prescription card company.

-135-

How can an employer decide whether to elect a prescription card plan?

Employees and dependents generally like the convenience of the card plan. The determining factor is usually cost and administration. Depending on the per-prescription deductible elected and the calendar-year deductible and coinsurance level of the health plan, a prescription card plan may be more expensive than standard reimbursement procedures. The employer also must consider the card distribution and *recovery* issue. For a company with a great deal of turnover, this process and the claims liability involved when cards are not recovered from terminated individuals may make a card plan more expensive than it looks, at first glance. (Claims submitted by a terminated individual who has retained the card will be paid by a card administrator if it has no record of employee termination.) Other loopholes for erroneous claims payment are also present in card plans. The employer should review with an intermediary the reputation of any card administrator the insurance company suggests.

-136-

Do health insurance plans cover dental care?

Proper dental care has been considered a budgetable expense not necessarily essential to good health, so traditionally, it has not been included in group health insurance plans. More recently, as its importance has become understood and its cost has increased, dental care has been added to employers' employee benefits plans. Some plans include dental as part of the medical plan; others include coverage as a separate plan. However, many health insurance plans do provide coverage for noncosmetic dental work necessary as the result of an accident. Some plans include limited coverage for hospital room and board coverage related to dental procedures, such as removal of impacted wisdom teeth, that are performed in a hospital.

-137-

How is vision care covered?

Most health insurance plans provide coverage for medical care related to eye injury or disease, but do not cover the costs of periodic eye examinations or corrective lenses. Like dental care, vision care is a relatively new employee benefit, offered by employers that can afford to expand their employee benefits plans to include additional fringe benefits previously considered budgetable. Vision care is most often covered on a scheduled basis that pays a fixed dollar amount for examinations, lenses, and frames.

-138-

What about coverage for hearing evaluations and hearing aids?

Like vision care, most health insurance plans provide coverage for medical care related to diseases or injury to the hearing mechanisms. They do not cover the cost of hearing evaluations or hearing aids to restore a person's ability to hear.

-139-

What types of benefits are generally not covered by a group health insurance plan?

Benefits that are generally not covered include those associated with procedures that are not medically necessary (for example, elective cosmetic surgery) and those that do not contribute materially to the treatment of a patient but that a patient can elect to use, such as hospital telephone and television charges. Also, in order to avoid duplicate payments, benefits that are available to an employee from another source, such as worker's compensation, are generally not covered.

Coverages that would create a substantial catastrophic risk that is considered beyond the scope of insurance are also excluded. For example, long-term nursing care has traditionally not been covered because of the unpredictability of the extent of the need for care and, hence, the inability of insurers to price the coverage. In addition, care required as a result of war and care that would normally not be charged for, such as care in certain state or federal hospitals, are not covered. Expenses for transportation are also not covered, except for specified ambulance services.

Routine physicals and other preventive care procedures have also not been covered traditionally, but some insurers now include a preventive care benefit.

-140-

What is preventive care coverage?

Preventive care coverage provides for expenses incurred in the prevention, rather than the treatment, of illness or injury. It is sometimes referred to as "well care." Some preventive care expenses have traditionally been covered, such as diagnostic tests to ascertain whether additional medication is required to control high blood pressure to *prevent* a stroke, and well baby care—nursery care and immunizations at birth. However, routine checkups for early detection of problems have not been covered.

-141-

What kinds of benefits does preventive care coverage provide when it is part of a health care plan?

Preventive care coverage can include a variety of benefits, ranging from routine checkups, immunizations, and Pap tests to health risk appraisals (HRAs) and wellness programs.

-142-

How often are routine checkups usually covered under a preventive care plan?

There is some difference of opinion in the medical profession concerning how often routine physical examinations should be conducted and how useful they are; therefore, there is a lack of uniformity regarding how often such exams are covered. Some plans cover them annually; others cover routine physicals as well as diagnostic tests and X-rays periodically, based on the insured's age.

-143-

What is a wellness program?

The most recent trend in preventive care is insurance coverage for HRAs and for exercise, nutrition, smoking cessation, and stress management programs. Because the programs encourage employees to achieve or maintain good health and well-being, they are commonly referred to as wellness programs.

Wellness programs are sometimes covered by insurance in larger companies whose claims experience significantly affects their health insurance premium rates (or when the employer is partially or fully self-funding the plan). However, some smaller employers are also being offered wellness insurance coverage as part of their plans.

-144-

Why would an employer want to include preventive care or wellness programs in a group insurance plan?

Some state laws mandate coverage, such as well baby care. A typical benefit covers nursery care for a fixed number of days and specific tests routinely done within 48 hours of birth. Some employers include other preventive care benefits because it is often cheaper to prevent an illness or injury than it is to treat it. Thus, by investing in programs that are designed to prevent illness, employers may realize future cost savings.

Another reason for including preventive care has to do with employees' increasing concern with their health. Employers looking to provide meaningful benefits to their employees can do so by providing preventive care coverage.

-145-

What is a health risk appraisal?

An HRA describes an individual's chances of death, illness, or injury in the future. A typical HRA asks the individual questions about his or her sex, age, family and individual health history, specific health practices, and life style (smoking, drinking alcohol, exercise, stress, seat-belt usage). Depending on the HRA, questions concerning the individual's reactions to everyday work and social situations may be included.

-146-

Would an employer include an HRA as part of a group health insurance plan?

Yes. By combining each employee's HRA scores, a total health risk profile of all employees can be produced. The employer will acquire significant information concerning the general health of the employee population in aggregate. Based on the information, the employer may decide to institute health programs or provide certain preventive care benefits. This will help employees improve their health, and may lead to cost savings to the extent medical care utilization is reduced.

-147-

Are HRA results used to set the price for health insurance coverage?

To date, this has not occurred. However, as society becomes less inclined to subsidize the health care expenses of individuals with controllable health risks, HRA-based premiums may begin to be used.

-148-

Do insurance companies provide financial incentives to companies to adopt preventive care programs?

Some insurance carriers provide financial incentives for purchasing preventive care programs. This can take the form of lower premium payments to employers that have the programs in place. Others provide deductible and coinsurance percentages related to employee health. For example, employees who control their weight and blood pressure, wear seat belts, do not smoke, and have periodic physical exams may have their annual deductible waived. Some insurance companies also provide for partial reimbursement for individuals who attend health or exercise programs.

-149-

Do most policies include an overall limit to the amount reimbursable to one individual?

Many policies have an overall lifetime limit. This is usually $1 million or $2 million. Some policies do not include an overall limit. Limits may be based on a calendar year or per illness or injury.

Most policies have a "reinstatement" provision that reinstates, or adds back, the dollar amounts that have been counted toward the lifetime maximum limit each year, usually on January 1. For example, if an insured incurs $35,000 of covered expenses during one year, $25,000 of that could be reinstated, meaning that only $10,000 counts toward the $1 million lifetime maximum.

Managing Health Insurance Costs

As health insurance costs have increased in recent years, insurers have redesigned their plans to include cost-containment features. This chapter explores the reasons behind rising health care costs and explains what some of these cost-containment features are and how they work.

-150-

What factors are responsible for rising health insurance costs?

There are two broad interrelated factors that have resulted in rising health insurance costs: the rising cost of health care services and an increase in the frequency of claims. The proliferation of new medical technologies, inappropriate use of medical services, an oversupply of medical professionals and facilities, high malpractice insurance rates, overall inflation, a payment system that insulates individuals from the true cost of care, and programs such as Medicare and Medicaid that require the private sector to pick up more than its true share of the cost of health care (known as "cost shifting") have all contributed to rising health care costs and increased utilization. Thus, the problem is widespread, and each party involved in the delivery of, consumption of, and payment for health care has contributed significantly to unbridled cost increases.

Health care providers—physicians, allied health practitioners, and health care facilities—have delivered a great deal of excellent, necessary medical care. They have also provided unnecessary care, and they have been allowed to price the care *after* it has been purchased.

Consumers have been increasingly insulated from the costs of medical care. Insurance has encouraged people to "buy" care without regard for its price. Many believe they are entitled to the best medical care available, whatever the cost. Individual responsibility for health has seemed unnecessary: Doctors have been regarded as the experts.

Insurance arrangements through private insurers, Blue Cross/Blue Shield (BC/BS), government programs, and employers' self-funded plans have insulated individuals from the cost of care. Expanding reimbursement parameters have been demanded by powerful employee groups such as organized labor, and have filtered to employees everywhere. Insurance companies, anxious to meet employers' and unions' demands, traditionally have delivered coverage with few cost controls.

-151-

Why haven't private insurance companies limited reimbursements to control cost increases?

When insurance companies have tried to limit reimbursement, individuals have been intolerant. For example, years ago, most health care plans covered a set number of days of hospital care. Patients with additional expenses were financially burdened. The demand for additional coverage was met by adding a major medical plan. More recently, an individual whose plan allowed only a set dollar amount for a certain surgical procedure was unhappy when the surgeon's charge exceeded that limit. Insurers responded to the demand for increased coverage by providing reasonable and customary (R&C) surgical reimbursement.

Attempts by insurers to market increased deductibles, coinsurance, and other benefits limitations have met with little positive response until recently. The demand has been for expanded coverage rather than for limits. Slowly, however, more limitations are being implemented by insurers, as a result of employers' demands for health insurance premium control.

-152-

Do Medicare and Medicaid limit reimbursement to achieve cost control?

Both programs have more limitations than private insurance or BC/BS coverages. Two kinds of reimbursement limitations—benefits restrictions and provider reimbursement restrictions—were intended to control costs, but have not.

The benefits restrictions limit the kinds of care and services that are covered. These are explained to insured individuals in their benefits booklets. The reimbursement restrictions are rules concerning the costs of care that Medicare and Medicaid will not recognize. That is, although coverage for an insured's hospital stay is provided by law, the hospital's charge for care cannot include the costs of:

- Bad debt and charity costs incurred in tracking patients who do not pay their bills;
- Some equity capital requirements associated with replacement and addition of facilities and equipment; and
- Teaching and research programs within the hospital.

The government did add a 2% load on the allowable charges to compensate for some of the reimbursement exclusions.

These government insurance programs also specify "reasonable" costs, similar to private insurers' R&C allowances, but the Medicare and Medicaid limits have become more conservative.

-153-

Why haven't the coverage limits of government programs controlled insurance costs?

Two factors have prevented cost control. First, reimbursement has been retrospective. When hospitals are not paid before delivering care, they are free to deliver whatever care is "needed," with little concern for the cost involved. Bills are submitted to private and public insurers, and paid. Second, the costs not subsidized by the government programs have been shifted to private payers.

Hospitals that received less reimbursement than the total cost of care in one year would finance this deficit through price increases. Higher prices didn't turn buyers away—private insurers simply paid for the care consumed as charged. Certain kinds of expensive care were zealously provided, leading to an increase in the consumption of care, which led to a need for additional facilities, followed by a need for financing, debt, and higher costs of care—which Medicare and Medicaid refused to pay. So hospitals continued to subsidize government insureds' care with private payers' money.

-154-

What is cost shifting?

Cost shifting is the term used to describe how one patient's health care is subsidized by the charges made to another for the same services. It occurs when the first patient's insurer has an arrangement, established by law or negotiation, that allows for reimbursement at less than the normal full charge. Medicare and Medicaid are examples of cost shifting arrangements created by law. Hospitals and physicians are faced with what they believe is less than adequate reimbursement for a large number of patients, which must be made up elsewhere. The providers shift costs to other patients, thus inflating the charges for the care delivered. BC/BS plans have created a similar situation through negotiation.

-155-

How do higher claims affect health insurance costs?

Health insurance premiums are based in part on the expected

number and cost of claims that will be filed during a plan year. If the actual number and cost of claims exceed the expected level, the insurer will probably increase future premiums to reflect the higher claims experience.

-156-

Why do health care providers deliver unnecessary care?

Most physicians and other practitioners do not *set out* to provide unnecessary care to their patients. However, they, as well as the facilities they practice in, are encouraged to do so, because:

- Demand for care is not price-driven;
- Patients traditionally have not questioned treatment; and
- Care deemed unnecessary by one physician may be deemed appropriate by another.

It should not be surprising that when no one questions the price or the quantity of care provided, and the quality of care is subjective, more care, rather than less, is "bought" and "sold." In any market, increased demand increases price. In the health care market, price increases have not, until recently, resulted in a corresponding decrease in demand for services.

-157-

Why haven't consumers purchased less care, as prices have increased?

Insurance companies reimburse individuals for health care expenses with relatively few restrictions on the price of the care received. Although, in reality, consumers are the payers, they fail to see it that way because they continue to receive care while sharing little in the cost. Further, consumers feel entitled to medical care. An increase in price, even if passed directly to consumers, does not result in the same relative decrease in demand that occurs in simpler markets.

-158-

How can a small employer manage health insurance costs?

Many factors affecting the rising cost of health care are beyond the scope of the small employer. However, small employers can manage their health insurance costs in several ways:

- Work-site programs that encourage employees to improve their health and educate them on prudent and effective use of health care;
- Benefits plan designs that encourage cost-effective consumption of health care; and
- Arrangements with health care providers, generally through an insurer, that control the price and quantity of care provided.

Combining cost-management techniques is usually necessary. For example, if an educational program encourages employees to obtain periodic physical examinations, the health insurance plan should be adjusted to reimburse individuals for that. Arranging for physicals and tests to be provided at a set price by a certain provider is one way to control the cost of this preventive care benefit.

-159-

Should employers that have not experienced large premium increases be concerned with cost management?

Yes. In this way, employers can help prevent future increases. Furthermore, as more employers assume responsibility for management of health plan costs, there should be an overall cost impact.

-160-

How can employers determine what cost management is required?

To determine the appropriate cost-management programs, the

employer must ascertain the specific problems that are causing the company's costs to rise. This involves analyzing the internal situation—an employer's own claims experience—as well as the external situation—the price and quality of the care delivered by providers in the local area.

Insurers have developed management information systems and reporting and analysis services that can provide employers with many of these cost data. These automated systems also provide the information that will allow insurers to suggest plan redesign and work with employers for direct intervention with physicians and hospitals.

-161-

What kinds of data are useful to better manage health care costs?

Useful data include several years of claims experience, presenting such detail as charges and allowed payments, broken down by diagnosis and health care provider.

Employers with fewer than 100 employees certainly have too low a claims volume to indicate conclusively what type of cost management is appropriate. This is why insurers offer many standard cost-controlling plan design features, even if specific claims problems are not clear. For example, appendectomies performed by one hospital may be clearly more expensive than the same procedure performed elsewhere. From the employer's claims information, it may appear that a certain physician orders more tests for a condition than another. Both situations indicate that the insured should be made aware of the differences so a more informed decision can be made.

However, unless an employer's claims volume is very high for specific conditions and for specific providers, conclusions may be inaccurate. For employers with fewer than 500 employees, conclusions about providers based on just their own claims analysis is dangerous. Additional data regarding provider practice patterns are necessary. These can be obtained from the employer's insurer or third-party administrator (TPA).

-162-

What kinds of plan design features should employers implement, even without conclusive data on problems?

Several specific actions can be taken to help manage costs, such as implementing plan features that:

- Prevent illness and injury;
- Increase cost sharing by employees; and
- Encourage utilization of the most cost-effective care.

-163-

What plan features prevent illness and injury?

Preventive care programs that pay for routine physical examinations and tests can help detect symptoms of illness early, and prevent its progression. Individuals who take advantage of covered physicals and tests may learn to take better care of themselves, as their physicians educate them on proper "well care" or preventive care strategies.

Other "wellness" programs, such as lower back care and nutrition workshops, can prevent injury and illness or improve an already existing condition. Programs for weight control, substance abuse, and smoking cessation can significantly affect employees' health and the eventual cost of the employer's health care plan. Employers are beginning to implement these kinds of programs—sometimes paying part of the cost to the employee either directly or through an insurance plan.

Many employers provide their employees with periodic health risk appraisals (HRAs) to help increase awareness and, over the long term, change employees' health-related behaviors in the hope that healthier employees (and their dependents) will result in higher morale and lower claims costs. HRAs are explained more fully at Questions 145–147.

-164-

How can a plan increase cost sharing by employees?

A cost-sharing increase does not, as used in this question, refer to an increase in the employee's contributions to premium, although some employers have found this necessary in recent years. Cost sharing refers to increases in the individual's cost when he or she consumes health care.

The simplest cost sharing is achieved through implementation of or increases to deductibles and coinsurance percentages. For example, base plus plans may be changed to comprehensive plans to implement deductibles and coinsurance on all health care expenses. Employers can implement deductible amounts ranging from $100 to $1,000 (or even higher) per individual per calendar year. Special deductibles for certain kinds of care, or for care related to one illness or injury, may also be applied, and deductibles may be based on employees' earnings.

Although a $100 deductible is still very common, a calendar-year deductible of $100 has little effect today on an individual's health care buying habits. Many employers have already increased their calendar-year deductibles to $200 or $250. In addition, they have waived or added deductibles for certain kinds of care to encourage cost-effective behavior. For example, an employer that wants employees to stay out of the hospital whenever possible may require that a hospital-per-admission deductible be added to the plan. This may be in addition to the regular $200 deductible.

An employer that adds a preventive care benefit to the plan may waive the regular annual deductible on that care to encourage employees to use it. The deductible may also be waived on outpatient services such as surgery and home health care to provide a financial incentive for their use. Conversely, an additional deductible may be required for unnecessary emergency room visits.

Deductibles based on earnings may be achieved by use of a schedule or a set percentage amount. Employees earning less than $20,000 a year may be subject to a $200 deductible; employees earning $20,000–$40,000 per year, $300; and employees earning more than

$40,000, $400. Or each employee may have his or her own deductible, figured as 1% or 1½% of salary, to a maximum of $600, for example. This adds complexity to the plan, and may cause dissatisfaction among the more highly paid employees. However, it does provide an equitable way to control costs that takes into account an individual's ability to pay.

Coinsurance percentages on both major medical and comprehensive plans are usually 20% for the employee, 80% for the insurance company. Some employers have changed to a 25%/75% split, or have decreased the employee's share when certain kinds of care are received. For example, a visit to an outpatient surgical center may be paid at 90% by the insurance company, while a hospital visit would be paid at 80%.

-165-

What is a front-end deductible?

A front-end deductible is a deductible that must be satisfied before any covered health insurance expense will be reimbursed. It is also commonly called a first-dollar deductible and is included in a "purely" comprehensive health insurance plan.

-166-

Do all comprehensive plans have front-end deductibles?

Some comprehensive plans do not require a front-end deductible for all covered health care expenses. Such plans most often have a full-pay hospital provision under which no deductible is required for reimbursement of hospital expenses. Employers add this because they believe that anyone who requires hospital confinement is seriously ill and should be reimbursed without a deductible or coinsurance. The employee, however, would have to satisfy the deductible before being reimbursed for any other covered health care expenses.

This type of plan design can encourage unnecessary hospitalization because care as an inpatient is financially advantageous. However, this can be controlled by also including a preauthorization review feature for all hospital confinements.

-167-

Would increases in required employee contributions toward premium help control costs?

There is a school of thought that believes employees who are asked to contribute more to health care coverage will feel more entitled to care, and may be less likely to be concerned about the cost and the quantity they purchase. However, if an increase in employee contributions is *suggested* to employees as a likelihood (if costs are not controlled soon), employees may be more responsive to benefit redesign as the alternative.

Some employers have not increased required employee contributions per se, but have offered employees choices in coverage by giving them a certain amount of benefits money to "spend" on annual premiums for various insurance coverages. These plans, called "cafeteria plans" or "flexible benefits plans," usually result in employees being more aware of the costs of care, because *they themselves* have made the decision about where to spend their benefits dollars and have elected medical coverage with increased deductibles and coinsurances. Further, some employers include a medical reimbursement account in their cafeteria plans. These accounts allow individuals to place money into the account through payroll deductions (on a pre-tax basis) to be used for medical care not covered by the health insurance plan. The money is perceived as their own money, and they usually spend it more wisely. It serves as a cushion that makes employees more comfortable with the idea of selecting a medical care plan with a higher deductible. See the chapter entitled "Flexible Benefits" for a more detailed discussion.

-168-

How can health care plans be designed to encourage use of the most cost-effective care?

Traditionally, coinsurance provisions have been the only incentive for individuals to seek less expensive care. However, their effectiveness is limited. Many individuals equate expensive care with quality care, and more care with better care. Physicians have encouraged "Cadillac" care because there was no incentive for them to recommend otherwise, for patients with insurance. As costs have increased, more effective cost-management features have been developed, including coordination of benefits, outpatient surgery coverage, preadmission testing, second surgical opinion programs, extended care facility coverage, home health care, hospital bill audit, and hospice care.

-169-

How does coordination of benefits help manage claims costs?

Coordination of benefits (COB) is a process by which insurers that cover the same individual for similar kinds of health care expenses coordinate their payments so that the insured is reimbursed for no more than the amount of the expense. When a claim is submitted and the insured is entitled to benefits for the same expense from more than one source, the benefits are coordinated among insurers. The employee usually cannot receive coverage for more than 100% of health care expenses. COB was initiated years ago, due to the rapid increase in overinsurance. COB saves between 4% and 9% in claims costs. Standard COB provisions are included automatically in almost all group health care plans.

While COB deals with the issue of duplicate coverage, flexible benefits plans (see the chapter entitled "Flexible Benefits") provide a more cost-effective way to deal with employees' diverse needs.

Such plans allow employees to choose only the benefits they need from a menu of benefits made available by the employer.

-170-

How does outpatient surgery coverage help control costs?

Outpatient surgery coverage helps reduce hospital admissions for procedures that can be performed safely in the outpatient department, in a freestanding surgicenter, or even in a doctor's office. These alternatives usually cost less. To encourage use of such alternatives, some plans provide better payment for outpatient surgery than they do for inpatient care. For example, the plan may waive the deductible for a surgicenter procedure or pay the bill at 100% instead of 80%. It is ironic that base plus major medical plans have made payment on exactly the opposite basis for years.

-171-

What is preadmission testing and how does it control costs?

Preadmission testing (PAT) results in shorter hospital stays. X-rays, lab tests, and examinations are done before the individual's hospital admission. Reimbursement is sometimes made on a more generous basis, such as at 100% payment or with no deductible, to encourage PAT.

Health insurance has encouraged hospital admission for these diagnostic tests by covering the days needed to perform the tests. Patients supposedly could become acclimated to the hospital before treatment, and doctors, as well as patients, found early admission sometimes more convenient; hospitals also wanted to keep their beds filled. But times have changed. Technological advances have made testing safe and efficient on an outpatient basis, people are becoming accustomed to treatment without "acclimation," and the costs involved in longer than necessary stays are of more concern than the convenience. Although hospitals, now more than ever, are struggling to keep their beds filled in order to keep revenues up, the cost of a hospital stay has finally increased enough to affect demand.

-172-

How would an employer encourage second surgical opinions through a health care plan?

Second surgical opinion (SSO) programs encourage individuals to have a second evaluation of the medical condition for which elective surgery has been recommended. Kinds of surgery for which SSOs are especially suggested, because there is evidence they are often performed unnecessarily, include:

- Adenoidectomy—removal of adenoids;
- Bunionectomy—removal of bunion (on the foot);
- Cataract extraction—removal of lens from eye;
- Cholecystectomy—removal of gallbladder;
- Coronary bypass—open-heart surgery;
- Excision of neuroma—removal of tumor of nerve fibers;
- Gastrectomy—removal of a portion of the stomach;
- Hemorrhoidectomy—removal of hemorrhoid;
- Herniorrhaphy—repair of hernia;
- Hip surgery;
- Hysterectomy—removal of uterus;
- Knee surgery;
- Laminectomy—removal of intervertebral disc of spine;
- Ligation and stripping of varicose veins—tying and removal of varicose veins of leg;
- Mammaplasty—plastic surgery on breasts;
- Menisectomy—removal of semilunar cartilage of knee joint;
- Myringotomy—incision into tympanic membrane of ear to drain fluid;
- Ocular muscle surgery for strabismus;

- Oophorectomy—removal of ovaries;
- Prostatectomy—removal of prostate;
- Reattachment of retina;
- Submucous resection—removal of submucous membrane from nasal septum;
- Thyroidectomy—removal of thyroid gland;
- Tonsillectomy—removal of tonsils; and
- Tympanoplasty—surgical repair of eardrum;

The decision to elect or reject surgery still remains with the patient.

Insurance reimbursement for an SSO has been available through many plans for years, but it has only been in the last several years that the coverage has been highlighted. Some plans provide SSO coverage and require no deductible or coinsurance for an SSO, or even a third surgical opinion, if the first two disagree. Other plans allow a set dollar amount for a second or third opinion.

-173-

How are mandatory SSO programs different from voluntary SSO programs?

Typically, a list of elective surgeries for which a second opinion must be obtained is included in the employee's health plan booklet. If an employee does not seek a second opinion and has the surgery, payments for the surgery are limited. For example, the coinsurance provision may be 50%/50% for the surgeon's bill. Some plans eliminate payment altogether.

Studies have shown that mandatory programs decrease surgery more effectively than voluntary programs. However, some employers are uncomfortable with programs that inhibit their employees' free choice or penalize them for choosing a certain type of care. Before implementing this kind of benefit, an employer must be certain of its willingness to defend the programs when employees are dissatisfied. It is also necessary to educate employees and their dependents about new plan features.

-174-

Why does coverage for extended care facilities and home health care help an employer manage health care costs?

The average cost for a day in a hospital varies from region to region and hospital to hospital, but it is almost always higher than for a day in an extended care facility. Many individuals can recuperate just as quickly and safely at a skilled nursing center, and hold costs down.

Home health care can be even less expensive. In addition, some patients find that recuperation at home is much more comfortable and faster than in a hospital. Further, spread of infectious disease in hospitals makes extended stays sometimes riskier than most people are aware of.

-175-

Why does the addition of a hospice care benefit help manage claims costs?

Hospice care is palliative, intended to relieve pain or symptoms rather than actually curing disease. It is provided to individuals with diseases that are incurable or have progressed to untreatable stages. Most hospice care benefits pay for additional home care, hospice facility care, palliative drugs and therapy, family counseling, and respite for family members caring for the patient.

This care has been shown to cost much less than confinement in an acute care hospital, where many chronically ill individuals spend much of their last several months. Traditional health care plans cover expenses for necessary medical care, aimed at curing illness or injury. Technically speaking, hospice care does not cure disease, and therefore clear-cut contractual coverage for palliative care is necessary in order for insurers to cover hospice care expenses.

-176-

If an employer determines that plan design features alone will not manage costs sufficiently, what other options are available?

A wide variety of techniques other than plan design features have been implemented to reduce the cost of health insurance plans. The most common of these are educational programs, hospital audits, negotiated arrangements with health care providers, utilization review, and some form of self-funding.

-177-

How does education contribute toward health care cost control?

Some employers have undertaken massive communications campaigns to educate their employees on the prudent purchase of medical care. Insurers often provide educational material to help employees understand their health insurance plans, and sometimes they help run educational meetings. The message for cost control comes best from the employer; employees will not respond as well to an insurer that suggests they purchase less or less expensive health care even when it is more appropriate. However, a plea by the president of a company may fall on receptive ears. Messages can be communicated quickly and effectively to smaller groups, and confusion can be dealt with immediately.

-178-

What is a hospital bill audit?

Hospital bill audits take two forms: audits done by an insurer or a professional bill review organization hired by the insurer, and audits by patients themselves. Professional bill audits involve retrospective review of all charges billed by a hospital, to ascertain whether all services for which charges are billed were delivered, and whether the charges are reasonable. Many hospital bills have errors, and insurers have found significant cost savings in questioning them. Audits are generally performed on larger bills, and the claimant and the hospital are put on notice that an audit is being performed, so that late payment is not an insured's problem.

Employee bill audits have been implemented recently at some companies. Employees are encouraged to review their own hospital bills, just as they would review car repair bills, before they pay them or submit them to their insurer for payment. Financial incentives help; some insurance companies will pay the person who discovers an error half of the amount of the billing error, up to a maximum amount per year. These programs may be worthwhile not only in helping insurance companies find billing errors, but also in educating individuals on the substantial costs of care.

-179-

How can negotiations with providers contribute toward cost management?

A more complex approach to cost management involves negotiations between insurance companies and health care providers. Large self-insured employers may become directly involved with providers, but most employers work through their insurers.

Preferred provider organizations (PPOs) are groups of health care providers—doctors, allied health practitioners, and hospitals—that contract with insurers (or large employers) to provide specified health care, sometimes at discount rates and always with strict utilization review. This contrasts with traditional insurance arrangements in which insurers did not negotiate prices with the providers; they simply paid the charges for the services performed in accordance with the contract. As has been discussed previously, both Blue Cross/Blue Shield (BC/BS) and Medicare/Medicaid negotiate price, to a degree, with providers. Recently, private insurers have become involved with PPOs to do so.

Typically, employers looking for cost management purchase a health care plan that gives employees an unlimited choice of health care providers, but when individuals use a "preferred provider," they are reimbursed at a more generous rate than they would have been had they been treated by a nonpreferred provider. Health care costs are managed for the employer in two ways: (1) the price for a plan that includes preferred providers is less expensive than one without, because the health care prices have been discounted; and (2) the preferred providers are contractually bound to give *appropriate* care. Utilization review is an integral part of preferred provider arrangements. PPOs are discussed in more detail in the following chapter, entitled "Alternative Health Care Systems."

-180-

What is utilization review?

A process called utilization review (UR) has been implemented by some insurers and employers in recent years. It evaluates the appropriateness, necessity, and quality of health care provided at various stages in its delivery. Although this feature is technically a part of health insurance plan design, it is different in that it analyzes whether the care prescribed and delivered is justifiable and appropriate. Other cost-management plan design features encourage cost-effective use of care, rather than try to manage care on an individual basis.

-181-

Exactly how does UR work?

UR offers some control over providers' decisions on what care to provide, and allows for retrospective review of care provided to uncover aberrant practice patterns among physicians. For years, insurance companies have retrospectively reviewed claims in order to catch charges or services that were inappropriate. UR is peer review—doctors analyzing other doctors' care, and some of it is done before or during delivery of care.

Employers can obtain UR services directly from a UR company, through a broker or TPA, or through the insurer. Numerous review companies are available to choose from, but their services are similar. The services usually focus on hospital review, but some UR agencies provide review of outpatient surgery, treatment of mental illness, and long-term care. The hospital review services usually consist of:

- Preadmission certification;
- Concurrent review with discharge planning; and
- Retrospective review.

-182-

How does preadmission certification work?

An employer that elects UR for its health plan explains to employees and their dependents that before any nonemergency hospital admission, the individual will be expected to contact the UR organization, or the medical care review agent, to obtain preadmission certification. The medical review agent will analyze the situation prior to the prescribed surgery or hospital stay. This watchdog function stimulates the attending physician to prescribe necessary, cost-efficient care and, when questioned, to justify surgical procedures or hospital stays with clear evidence of patient need. Failure by the insured to initiate the process usually results in reduced payment for treatment even if it would have been certified if reviewed. Emergency admissions are to be reported for review usually within 48 hours of admission.

This idea is not new: In the 1950s, several unions asked medical societies to help them conserve dollars in their health and welfare funds by reviewing health care services received by their members. Medicare spawned foundations for medical care (FMCs) in the early 1960s, and later, 200 professional standards review organizations (PSROs) were created to provide for review of all federally financed patient care in acute care hospitals, with plans to extend review to long-term care and ambulatory care services in later years.

Recently, private insurers have incorporated UR into their benefits services.

An individual contemplating a hospital admission may not deal with the medical review agent after the first call or letter. The agent often deals directly with the attending physician in order to get a clear understanding of the reasons for the admission. The agent either confirms the need for the admission; suggests an alternative setting, such as an outpatient facility; or suggests that the surgery or treatment is inappropriate, and that an alternative be explored. A second surgical opinion may be requested. In any situation in which an intake nurse reviews the plan of care and does not agree with it, he or she passes the case to an M.D., who then attempts to reach an agreement with the attending physician as to the appropriate care. If the two physicians disagree, usually a second UR physician reviews the plan of care. If the UR organization still disagrees with the patient's physician after that second review, and the patient goes ahead with the admission, the employer's insurer will either pay the claim as usual, or reduce the benefit percentage. The course of action depends on the arrangement agreed upon when UR is implemented as part of the insurance plan. Employees receive materials explaining the claims payment implication involved before the UR process takes effect.

The review process is fully documented, and the information is provided to the insurer as well as the attending physician and the patient. Most often, the hospital admission is approved, and the person is admitted as planned. The review process then continues with concurrent review.

-183-

If hospital admissions are usually certified, why is UR necessary?

Although it is difficult to prove, it appears that UR has a sentinel effect on physicians. That is, physicians who are told by their patients that the hospital admission must be precertified are more likely to suggest an alternative to hospitalization if there is one. The presence of the program alone may be as valuable as the actual reviews.

-184-

What happens during concurrent review?

Patients' care is monitored while they are in the hospital. The UR organization may send a nurse on site, or communicate with the physician or physician's assistant by telephone to keep abreast of the length of the stay. Less frequently, other procedures and services are audited. Concurrent review is aimed at getting the patient out of the hospital as quickly as possible, with due regard to patient safety.

Patients are often kept an extra day or two even though they can be discharged safely if home care or extended care at a more appropriate facility can be arranged. Concurrent review allows the discharge planning process to begin as soon as possible after the patient is admitted. Some hospitals have been slow to discharge privately insured patients because they subsidize other patients' hospital stays. It has also been easier for a physician to decide to keep a patient than to risk the repercussions if a patient is sent home too early. Malpractice suits remind physicians to practice conservatively.

-185-

How does retrospective review help manage claims costs?

The UR organization typically provides the insurer (or large employer) with periodic reports on physicians' practice patterns and hospitals' length-of-stay averages. In areas where there are several providers to choose from, the providers who consistently deliver cost-effective care can be identified and insureds can be channeled to them. In regions with only one hospital and a handful of doctors, discussions can at least be opened with that institution and those physicians to review patterns of care. Information that will help alter practice patterns may be a sensitive issue, but such discussions are being held frequently, as insurers and employers pursue cost management.

-186-

Do the cost savings produced by UR justify the additional expense for the UR service?

Experience of plans that have had UR in effect long enough to evaluate indicates that savings exceed the cost, resulting in a 3% to 10% reduction in overall premium. The key to getting the most from the effort is a clear explanation to employees of the process and its purpose.

Alternative Health Care Systems

The preceding chapter discusses ways to manage health care costs by adding plan design features such as second surgical opinions, outpatient surgery incentives, and utilization review. These approaches encourage more responsible health care consumption by consumers. Another cost-management option available to employers is to reorganize the way in which their employees' health care services are provided and paid for. This chapter discusses alternative health care delivery and reimbursement systems such as health maintenance organizations and preferred provider organizations.

-187-

How has the traditional reimbursement system in this country contributed to the escalating cost of health care?

Retrospective reimbursement guarantees revenues to doctors and hospitals. There are few financial incentives for providers to reduce the amount of care or to deliver it more efficiently because in most plans payment and reimbursement are on a fee-for-service basis. More care generally means more revenue. Patients have allowed this to occur because they have been insulated from the cost of care through their insurance plans. There are minimal financial barriers to getting as much care as desired.

Broad insurance coverage encourages employees to use medical care with little regard for price. The system suggests that more care is better, and that employees should not worry about the cost of the care. Demand for care does not drop as price increases, and insurance companies have passed along the costs of increased utilization and cost of care to employers in the form of annual premium rate increases.

-188-

What is being done to control health care costs?

Employers, through the implementation of cost-management health care plans, are attempting to continue to make quality care available to their employees at a reduced cost to themselves. Insurers—the government, Blue Cross/Blue Shield (BC/BS), and private companies—are trying to accommodate their policyholders by finding innovative, cost-effective ways to design and administer plans; legislators are trying to respond to the public's demand for affordable care. However, the most significant upheaval involves the providers of care. Through a variety of arrangements with insurers and employers, providers are reorganizing their delivery approaches to maintain their market share in a world where, suddenly, uncontrolled consumption of care is not as acceptable as in prior years.

-189-

How are insurers and providers merging their services?

In essence, employers and their insurers—the government, BC/BS, and private insurers—have determined that too much money is being spent on health care. Insurers cannot simply restrict reimbursement of reasonable and customary (R&C) charges to reduce costs. Further, providers—particularly hospitals—are experiencing decreasing demand for their services due to alternative care facilities and insurance plans that channel insureds to the least expensive care sites. As a result, insurers have begun working with providers to reorganize the delivery of care. Providers and insurers are exchanging roles. Insurers are becoming involved in defining reimbursable delivery of health care, and providers are entering into risk- and profit-sharing arrangements with insurance companies. Two well-defined models of integrated service are health maintenance organizations (HMOs) and preferred provider organizations (PPOs).

-190-

What is an HMO?

An HMO is an organization that provides comprehensive health care to a voluntarily enrolled population at a predetermined price. Members pay fixed, periodic (usually monthly) fees directly to the HMO and in return receive health care service as often as needed. This payment structure is known as a "capitative" payment structure.

HMO revenues increase only when enrollment increases, not when services increase. If monthly payments from members exceed the funds the HMO expends on care, the HMO profits. If revenues are less than the cost of care, the HMO loses.

-191-

How is a "capitative" payment structure different from a "fee-for-service" payment structure?

Health care providers—which include both individuals (e.g., medical doctors, dentists, osteopaths, psychiatric social workers, physical therapists, and chiropractors) and institutions (hospitals, clinics, surgicenters, skilled nursing care facilities, and hospices)—have historically been compensated on a fee-for-service basis each time service is provided. A doctor examines a patient complaining of back pain and is compensated for that examination. A hospital provides emergency room care to a heart attack victim and is paid for the treatment provided. A capitative payment structure, however, is one in which services are paid for in advance on a per-person basis without knowing whether any service will be required. This prepaid arrangement is analogous to a person buying an annual maintenance warranty program without knowing whether the washing machine will ever need repair. Care on a prepayment basis requires insignificant cost sharing beyond the fixed prepayment fee.

-192-

Do employers prepay for health care services on traditional plans?

In a sense, employers "prepay" for expenses their employees will incur by agreeing to pay fixed monthly health care premiums to an insurer. Although premiums are prepaid, *providers* are paid on a fee-for-service basis.

-193-

Do employees prepay for health care by way of their payroll deductions for traditional plans?

To a degree, employees do prepay for their medical care. Many employees (particularly those under a base plus major medical plan, whose hospital expenses may be paid at 100% with no deductible) perceive their health care costs to be on a prepaid basis, because their monthly contributions are fixed payroll deductions. However, for expenses covered under major medical and comprehensive plans, employees do share in the cost of each service as it is provided, in addition to the monthly premiums paid.

-194-

Does enrollment in an HMO entitle an individual to unlimited health care?

Care under HMO plans is very comprehensive and includes both physician and hospital services. Enrollment in an HMO entitles the individual to as much future health care service as needed, but there are limitations on the extent of that service, just as there are restrictions on the care allowable under other health plans. For example, cosmetic surgery would generally not be covered by an HMO plan.

-195-

Who develops and sponsors HMOs?

HMOs have several different types of sponsors. Some have been developed and sponsored by employers and/or labor unions. Others have been started by medical schools, hospitals, or medical clinics. Some insurance companies have also been involved in establishing their own HMOs or have invested capital or in-kind expertise in existing or developing organizations.

-196-

Do HMOs require a deductible that patients pay before care is provided?

Some HMOs require members to pay only periodic membership fees. However, many HMOs have recently begun to require a small per-visit deductible or charge in addition to the membership payments.

-197-

How are HMOs organized?

HMOs are organized on a physician basis. There are four basic organizations of HMO physicians:

(1) The group model;
(2) The staff model;

(3) The network model; and
(4) The independent practice association (IPA) model.

-198-

What are the differences among the various models?

Interstudy, the leading HMO analysis organization, provides the following definitions:

(1) *Group model:* An HMO that contracts with one independent group practice to provide health services. Care is usually billed to the HMO on a fee-for-service basis.

(2) *Staff model:* An HMO that delivers health services through a physician group that is controlled by the HMO unit. The physicians, in effect, are employed and paid by the HMO.

(3) *Network model:* An HMO that contracts with two or more independent group practices (no solo practices) to provide health services.

(4) *IPA model:* An HMO that contracts with physicians from various settings (a mixture of solo and group practices) to provide health services.

-199-

What happens when an individual who is enrolled in an HMO needs to be hospitalized?

Some HMOs lease or own hospitals to provide care to their members. Others simply negotiate arrangements with hospitals to provide the HMO members with hospital services.

-200-

Do physicians usually own HMOs?

Most HMOs require too much development and working capital

to be owned exclusively by physicians. HMOs are owned by major employers (such as John Deere, which developed an HMO primarily for its own employees), private insurance companies, hospitals, and various investors. Physicians typically have "pieces of the pie" under profit-sharing arrangements or partial ownership of the corporations. Therefore, they are inclined to provide the most cost-effective care. This contrasts with physicians in the traditional fee-for-service delivery system, who can increase their income by delivering *more* care.

-201-

When were HMOs developed?

Although HMOs have existed since 1929, the real impetus to their development came in 1970. It was then that the federal government, as part of its continual evaluation of the health care delivery system, recognized that the concept of prepaid health plans might correct structural, inflationary problems with fee-for-service health care.

The government was impressed with the health care delivery plan created by the Kaiser Aluminum Company. The plan was a combination insurer-provider for workers building the Grand Coulee Dam. The government was interested in the approach because Kaiser was providing its workers with quality health care for considerably less than it cost under traditional plans. The reduced costs were attributable in part to a decrease in utilization. The rate of hospitalization at that time was 349 days per 1,000 members per year, compared with a national average of 1,149 days per 1,000. The plan's emphasis on preventive care and its prepayment basis concept, which the government believed would encourage physicians to be more cost-conscious in their delivery of care, seemed to be working.

Congress later passed the HMO Act of 1973 to encourage the development of HMOs. It set requirements for federal qualification and provided for grants and loan guarantees for planning, development, and initial operating costs for those HMOs that met the qualifying standards. The Act also encouraged enrollment among a skeptical public by establishing criteria for HMOs seeking federal qualification. Only federally qualified HMOs are eligible for federal funding.

-202-

What standards must a federally qualified HMO meet?

To be federally qualified, an HMO must be organized and operated according to the law and provide health services as prescribed by the law. These include certain "basic health services," such as:

- Physician services (including consultant and referral services by a physician);
- Inpatient and outpatient hospital services;
- Medically necessary emergency health services;
- Short-term (maximum 20 visits) outpatient evaluative and crisis intervention mental health services;
- Medical treatment and referral services (including referral services to appropriate ancillary services) for the abuse of or addiction to alcohol and drugs;
- Diagnostic laboratory services and diagnostic and therapeutic radiological services;
- Home health services; and
- Preventive health services, including:
  (a) Immunizations,
  (b) Child care from birth,
  (c) Periodic health evaluations for adults,
  (d) Voluntary family planning services,
  (e) Infertility services, and
  (f) Children's eye and ear examinations to assess the need for vision and hearing correction.

A qualified HMO may also make available "supplemental health services" as specified in the law, including:

- Services of facilities for intermediate and long-term care;
- Vision care not included as a basic health service;
- Dental services not included as a basic health service;
- Mental health services not included as a basic health service;

- Long-term physical medicine and rehabilitative services (including physical therapy);
- Prescription drugs prescribed in the course of the provision by the HMO of a basic health service, or of one of the preceding supplemental health services; and
- Other health services, not included as basic health services, which have been approved by the Secretary of the Department of Health and Human Services.

Generally, a federally qualified HMO must charge its members a fixed fee under a community rating system.

-203-

What is a community rating system?

Under a community rating system, one average premium rate is determined on the basis of the entire membership's characteristics and past claims experience. This is different from the rate setting on private insurance plans, where a particular group's rates can be partially or fully based on *that group's* risk characteristics (age, sex, industry) and past claims experience.

-204-

What is the dual choice mandate?

The HMO Act of 1973 requires employers with 25 or more employees employed within the service area of a federally qualified HMO to offer their employees the option of selecting a federally qualified HMO as an alternative to the employer's conventional health insurance plan. The Act set forth certain procedures that HMOs must follow in order to be in compliance with the dual choice mandate. Once each year, employees must be given the choice to enroll either in the employer's health care plan or in a qualified HMO. To enroll employees, the HMO must make a formal written application to the employer, explaining the details of the HMO plan, at least 180 days before the anniversary date of the existing health plan. The employer is only required to offer one individual practice association and one group or staff model, even if more than one of each applies for recognition by the employer.

-205-

Is an employer that self-insures required to offer dual choice?

Yes. Federal regulations stipulate that any company (1) employing an average of 25 or more employees, (2) paying minimum wage, and (3) offering a health benefits plan to employees, must offer dual choice. (Retirees eligible for health benefits do not have to be counted toward the 25-employee minimum.) Self-funded plans are included as health benefits plans, which are defined as "any arrangement for the provision of, or payment for, any of the basic and supplemental health benefits specified in the law and towards which the employer makes a contribution that is offered to eligible employees and their eligible dependents, by or on behalf of an employing entity."

-206-

How prevalent are federally qualified HMOs?

In 1984, over one half of the HMOs were federally qualified, accounting for 81% of the total HMO membership.

-207-

Would an employee want to enroll in both a traditional plan and an HMO plan?

No. Enrolling in two plans would provide duplicate coverage, and the employee would pay premium/membership fees under two plans. Further, most insurers do not allow employees enrolled in an HMO to enroll in a traditional health plan as well.

-208-

Is an employer required to pay for HMO coverage for its employees?

Generally, the law requires that the employer contribute the same dollar amount for an employee who joins an HMO as would be paid for that employee to enroll in the employer's conventional health insurance plan. If the HMO is more expensive, the employee is required to pay the difference in order to enroll, although there are various employer approaches to this situation.

The required contribution to employees' HMO enrollment is sometimes not as straightforward as this simple principle. The HMO regulations allow two approaches for the contribution determination, recognizing differences in the way the rates for the traditional health coverage are developed. This determination of the necessary contribution should be made with the aid of the employer's insurer or the HMO involved.

-209-

How prevalent are HMOs?

According to the Interstudy 1984 National HMO Census, there were 428 HMO plans with a total of 16,742,630 members in 43 states, Guam, and the District of Columbia. Most HMOs are concentrated in major metropolitan areas since they need to draw on a large population base. California has the highest concentration of plans (30) and the largest enrollment (5.6 million). A breakdown of other highly concentrated states follows:

State	*Number of Plans*	*Members*
New York	12	1,304,387
Michigan	18	757,549
Illinois	18	715,150
Massachusetts	19	704,852
Wisconsin	27	684,220
Ohio	18	590,887
Florida	20	519,873

-210-

What role has federal funding played in the development of HMOs?

Although early HMO development, propelled by substantial federal funding, was relatively rapid, growth slowed during the period 1976–1982. However, with the recent increased emphasis on cost management and changes in delivery systems, enrollment in HMOs is increasing at record levels. Even as federal funding is reduced, leaving some HMOs near bankruptcy, enrollment continues to grow.

-211-

Why are some HMOs having financial difficulty?

HMO failures during the early 1980s were generally the result of undercapitalization, severe inflation leading to high medical care costs, slow membership enrollment, and inexperienced management. Without a sufficient spread of risk—number of members—a period of uncontrolled inflation can wreak havoc for insurers and health care providers. The HMO, a unique combination of medical care and risk management, is extremely difficult to manage successfully.

-212-

Are HMOs subject to state regulations?

Many states have laws meant to promote HMO development while ensuring the quality of care the HMO delivers. These laws also provide for grievance procedures for enrollees and allow for some form of enrollee participation in the HMO's policy-making body. Also, some states have established financial reserve requirements for HMOs that are similar to those required by insurance companies, or they require state approval of an HMO's rates. These laws vary from state to state. Minnesota law, for example, includes a provision that all companies with 100 or more employees who reside in Minnesota must offer HMO coverage to those employees even if the employer does not offer an existing health plan.

-213-

Why has enrollment in HMOs increased during the health care cost crisis?

Some employers are encouraging their employees to enroll in an HMO in their area if the cost of the HMO would be less than what the employer is currently spending on conventional plans or if the annual increase in membership payments is likely to be lower than the expected increase in insurance premiums. In addition, HMOs are increasingly attractive to employees who must pay for part of their health care costs. Since employers are increasing deductibles and coinsurance, some employees have found the HMO more attractive. (Some HMOs have cost-sharing provisions, but they generally are far less significant than conventional deductible and coinsurance amounts.)

-214-

Why might employers experience lower costs with HMOs than with other health care plans?

HMOs emphasize preventive care, and they minimize hospitalization by treating patients on an outpatient basis whenever possible. The financial structure of HMOs rewards physicians for providing the most cost-effective care. This strategy helps control the rate of hospital admissions and the length of hospital stays.

On average, the number of inpatient days per 1,000 individuals per year is considerably lower in HMOs than under traditional health care plans. Various studies have shown that HMOs' inpatient days per 1,000 members range from 50% to 75% of traditional fee-for-service group health plans. Since hospital costs make up the largest part of health care costs, HMO costs have tended to be lower, in aggregate, than those under traditional health care plans. In addition, there is evidence that HMOs attract younger and perhaps heathier people who would require, on average, less medical care than older persons.

However, as traditional health plans have changed to provide for cost management, rates of hospitalization and lengths of stays have begun to decrease under those plans as well. Costs of HMOs versus those of other providers may become comparable as additional efficiency is introduced into the traditional health care delivery system, and as HMOs cover a broader cross section of the population.

-215-

Why might HMOs attract younger, healthier persons?

One reason may be that HMOs require members to receive care from a limited group of physicians. Younger persons are generally less likely to be attached to one doctor. Also, younger persons tend to be less concerned than their elder counterparts about experiencing serious illness, and their choice of medical plans may reflect this attitude. Younger persons may also be more willing to try new types of health care plans. The HMO care model is a relatively new concept, and older persons may question the quality of care. However, HMOs have begun to enroll more older members since Medicare began allowing its insureds the option of belonging to an HMO.

-216-

How does the quality of HMO care compare with that of conventionally insured medical care?

There are no conclusive data that show HMOs provide better or worse care than traditional medical delivery systems. It is clear that HMO members see their doctors more frequently than conventionally insured individuals, and are admitted to hospitals less often, but no conclusion concerning the quality of care can be drawn from these findings. Less care does not necessarily mean poorer quality care, and more care does not suggest better care. Surveys indicate that some individuals are more satisfied with HMOs than their conventionally insured counterparts are with their medical plans, and others are less satisfied.

-217-

Who can join an HMO?

HMOs are open to all individuals, assuming of course that there is an HMO in their community. Certain limitations apply to new enrollees for treatment of conditions that existed prior to their enrollment, but evidence of insurability (E of I) is generally not required.

-218-

When can employees enroll in an HMO?

Employees can enroll in an HMO immediately upon employment instead of enrolling in the employer's plan. Employees can also leave the employer's plan at any time to enroll in the HMO, but then must provide the HMO with E of I. Or, they can wait until the specified period of open enrollment required under the dual choice mandate. The mandate specifies that once a year employees are allowed their choice, without providing E of I, of either a federally qualified HMO or the conventional insurance plan.

-219-

How does an employee choose whether to enroll in an HMO or in the traditional health plan?

When deciding whether to choose an HMO or a conventional health care plan, employees weigh the advantages and disadvantages of both. Generally, employees who join HMOs do so for one or more of the following reasons:

- The credentials and quality of care are well-established;
- The selection of doctors is broad enough to meet their needs;
- The location of the HMO is near their home or work;
- The HMO's office hours include late evenings and holidays, and it offers a 24-hour emergency on-call service;
- The individuals are agreeable to being treated for some conditions by a paraprofessional (e.g., a nurse practitioner or other non-medical doctor, whom some HMOs rely on heavily);
- HMO specialists to whom patients are referred are of high quality;
- HMOs require no claims forms; and
- The price is comparable to or less than the price of the regular group plan.

-220-

Are HMOs more cost-effective for employees?

Yes and no. Employees usually pay less for care once they are enrolled in the HMO, because there are few or no copayments or deductibles required. However, if employees receive care from non-HMO providers, neither the employer nor the HMO is required to pay their expenses. The HMO physicians determine medically appropriate care, and if a member does not agree with that determination and wishes to receive unauthorized care, he or she must pay for all the expenses associated with that care.

-221-

Will the cost of an employer's conventional plan be affected by an HMO plan?

If an employer loses half of its employees to an HMO, the employer's rates on a conventional plan may be higher than if all employees were enrolled. There is some evidence that suggests that the younger, healthier employees are more inclined to enroll in an HMO than their older, less healthy counterparts (see Question 215). Premium rates charged by insurance companies reflect the characteristics of a group. The size, "average" sex, and average age of the group will be affected when certain employees join an HMO. So, for example, if the group is older because young employees enrolled in the HMO, the premium rates would be higher.

-222-

How can an employer achieve 75% participation in its conventional plan if employees are allowed to enroll in HMOs?

The 75% requirement uses *eligible* individuals as a basis. Employees enrolled in an HMO generally are not eligible to participate in the employer's plan.

-223-

Is an employee reimbursed for care received outside the HMO area?

If an HMO member receives *emergency* care from a non-HMO provider, usually the member's HMO will pay the cost of the care. If an individual elects to receive nonemergency care from a non-HMO provider, the cost of this care is not reimbursable.

-224-

Besides HMOs, what other health care delivery alternatives are available?

The latest alternative is the preferred provider organization (PPO). PPOs are arrangements whereby a third-party payer, such as an insurance company, contracts with a group of medical care providers that agrees to furnish services at negotiated fees in return for prompt payment and a certain volume of patients. The medical care providers are usually groups of hospitals and physicians (and sometimes other health care practitioners). Besides insurers, the third-party payers can be large employers and third-party administrators (TPAs). The nature of the contracts and the parties to them are diverse.

-225-

What is a PPA, and how is it different from a PPO?

A PPA is a preferred provider *arrangement*. It refers to an *agreement* between health care providers and another entity or group of entities (insurance companies, employers, TPAs) to provide medical care services at negotiated fees to certain groups in return for prompt payment and increased patient volume. A PPO typically indicates an *actual organization* of providers, while a PPA suggests simply that a contractual agreement has been made, but there is no other legal entity formed as a result of the agreement. The providers enter into a contract directly with the insurer, employer, or TPA. (The term PPA can be used to describe a PPO arrangement itself, and is sometimes used interchangeably with the term PPO. This text uses PPO.)

-226-

How is the PPO concept different from BC/BS and Medicare contracts with providers?

With respect to discounting charges, it is not very different. For years, individuals covered under the BC/BS plans have had the option of receiving care from a participating or a nonparticipating physician or hospital. Charges of participating providers are covered more fully because of agreements between the providers and BC/BS and Medicare. Commercial insurers have only recently entered this negotiated price and service arena, in the form of PPOs.

PPOs, however, focus less on price discounts than on *managed care.* One significant weakness in BC/BS provider-insurer contracts has been the lack of utilization review (UR) and case management. Prices for care were discounted to BC/BS, but the amount of care was not managed. Thus, providers sometimes sought to make up for the agreed-to discounts by providing more care, on a fee-for-service basis, than might have been necessary. PPOs, however, include stringent utilization controls, agreed to by the providers and monitored by the insurance company or other party to the agreement.

-227-

Must a PPO include UR controls?

Each PPO developer is at liberty to structure the rules for the preferred providers' practice patterns as it sees fit. For instance, if an insurer decides to contract with various physicians in an area simply by negotiating a 5% discount to the providers' traditional fees for a two-year period, this is a PPA, and it does not have to include utilization control parameters.

This scenario is plausible, but unlikely. The effectiveness of the PPO in managing health care costs depends on the incentives for the PPO providers to deliver cost-effective care. Fee discounts alone will not provide this. The vast majority of PPOs, therefore, include stringent UR controls.

-228-

How does a PPO differ from an HMO?

An employee who joins an HMO must receive health care from the HMO doctors in order to have his or her expenses covered. Typically, a PPO is one *part* of an insurance plan, and each time an insured seeks health care, he or she has the choice of receiving it from a preferred provider or from any other provider. The individual is reimbursed on a more generous basis for the services of a preferred provider, but his or her expenses are still reimbursable in accordance with the plan if a nonpreferred provider is selected.

HMOs operate on a prepaid capitative basis; PPOs operate on a fee-for-service basis. That is, when a PPO is included in a health insurance plan, the employer pays its insurance company fixed monthly premiums, and each visit to a provider is paid for through the traditional reimbursement mechanism.

-229-

Are there federally qualified PPOs?

No. HMOs needed federal funding and support to develop, and the HMO Act of 1973 provided that. The PPO concept emerged from the marketplace with no legislative impetus and, to date, there is no set of national standards for PPOs.

-230-

Do state PPO standards or laws exist?

Yes. Many states have passed or proposed laws. The laws vary from enabling legislation, which simply notes that PPOs are pro-competitive and desirable, to laws that include specific discrimination tests for PPOs. Some states require that benefit payment differences be only a certain variance between non-PPO and PPO provider. Other laws include provisions that prohibit discrimination by classes of employees in terms of PPO versus non-PPO benefit payment percentages.

-231-

What is an exclusive provider organization?

An exclusive provider organization (EPO) closely resembles an HMO and is a type of PPO that requires individuals to use only designated preferred providers. An individual must decide whether he or she wishes to obtain services from preferred providers at the beginning of the plan year. For that year, services of nonpreferred providers are not reimbursable. Payment to providers is on a fee-for-service basis.

-232-

What are the incentives for doctors and hospitals to be preferred providers?

Hospitals and admitting doctors believe that by participating in a PPO they can expect to increase their market share by increasing patient volume. Because competition for patients is fierce, providers are willing to negotiate discounts in return for insurers helping to ensure increased patient volume. In addition, hospitals are now being forced to manage their delivery of care, and PPOs provide hospital administrators with a method to gauge and measure practice patterns and cost of care.

-233-

Can an insurer or employer establish its own PPO?

Yes. To do this, insurers and employers would establish their own guidelines for determining those providers to be included in the arrangement, and contract with the appropriate physicians and hospitals. Due to the complexities of today's health care system and antitrust laws, insurers seeking to create their own PPOs require the services of professionals with strong health care and legal backgrounds.

-234-

What is involved in establishing a PPO?

No matter who establishes a PPO, certain steps are involved. The complexities of merging medical care with insurance make these alternative delivery systems difficult to develop successfully.

First, an adequate network of health care providers must be determined. The locations of providers selected and the various specialties required will depend on the characteristics of the group for whom PPO care is to be provided. For example, if an employer with 50,000 employees is developing a PPO, the demographics of the group and their past medical care utilization should be reviewed in order to determine the types and numbers of providers that will be needed to meet the needs of that population. If the group health plan covers retirees, several geriatric specialists would be required; if the insured group includes a large percentage of dependent children, the number of pediatricians that should be available as preferred providers must be carefully determined.

After the spread of providers is determined, a plan for getting the best providers must be developed. This involves two crucial ingredients for a successful PPO: selecting physicians whose practice patterns are cost-effective and whose abilities are excellent, and providing the right incentives to encourage those physicians to become a part of the PPO. An intense review of practice patterns is usually performed to determine the appropriate physicians, and because of the expertise required to interpret these patterns, established health care consultants are normally used to perform this function.

While the historical practice patterns of the physicians will be expected to continue if they become part of the PPO, it is still necessary to develop the UR controls that will help ensure cost-effective medical care from the PPO physicians and hospitals. Therefore, as the ideal list of physicians is developed, a UR plan must be developed concurrently. This plan depends on the readiness of the providers (particularly the hospital management involved) to practice by the UR standards, and must be developed jointly with the providers involved. Later, as additional providers become part of the PPO, they will be required to subscribe to the UR that is a fundamental tenet of the PPO.

In addition to the actual medical practices of physicians, the accreditation, licensure, hospital staff privilege arrangements, appropriate liability and malpractice insurance, and other administrative details must be arranged.

Data-processing systems that will allow the care provided to be tracked are absolutely necessary to ensure that the most cost-effective treatment is provided. Hospitals unable to collect and produce these data in a form capable of analysis would not usually participate in a PPO.

Negotiating the price discounts that physicians and hospitals will provide to PPO participants is also done during the development of the provider network. The financial incentives that will encourage the providers to become involved vary, according to the medical marketplace at that time. A certain hospital may be willing to provide a discount of 10% to their per-diem rate for PPO insureds. A hospital with a large number of empty beds and a need to fill them may be willing to discount its surgical fees and its room and board fees.

Developing a mix of providers who will offer high-quality medical care but who also are willing to discount their fees requires a great deal of negotiation and administration. Months of negotiations are usually necessary to get the appropriate providers, a workable UR system, and discounted prices for medical services provided.

-235-

What antitrust issues affect PPO development and negotiations?

The relevant antitrust issue involved is price fixing. The fact that PPOs may eliminate competition because the same discounted fees are negotiated with many insurers (or employers or TPAs) may be construed as price fixing, which is a violation of antitrust law. However, the current stance among regulatory agencies is to *enable* PPO activity, mindful of, rather than confined by, the principles of antitrust law.

-236-

What incentives do employers have to include PPOs in their health plans?

PPOs allow employers to provide employees with health care

benefits at lower costs than traditional plans and, also, provide some relief to employers faced with unbridled annual premium increases. The cost savings come from the price discounts and utilization review negotiated with the preferred providers. Discounts to conventional premiums range from 5% to 20%.

-237-

What kinds of employers could expect the largest discounts from a PPO health plan?

Employers whose claims utilization patterns show that employees have been receiving a great deal of care from high-priced providers are the best candidates for big premium savings. The incidence of claims must be significant enough for a change in utilization to have a positive effect on the plan.

If an employer is located in an area with strong competition among health care providers, an insurer can probably negotiate a large discount on hospital room and board rates at certain area hospitals. These savings can be passed along to the employer.

If the employer's work force is concentrated in one area, the chances of channeling employees to certain designated hospitals are better, and the cost savings more likely. Only the more sophisticated PPOs include hospitals in many geographically dispersed areas.

-238-

How can employers encourage employees to use preferred providers?

A typical PPO plan pays a larger percentage of the insured's expenses when he or she visits a preferred provider. This is achieved by varying the deductibles and coinsurance on the plan. For example, some employers elect to retain the standard deductible and coinsurance for nonpreferred providers but to decrease them for expenses associated with a preferred provider visit. This is sometimes referred to as an "incentive plan." Other employers keep the plan deductible and coinsurance level for the preferred provider reimbursement, and increase the employee's share for nonpreferred provider care. This is referred to as a "punitive plan." Other employers use a combination of both methods.

Employer Payment Structures with PPO

	Non-PP Care	*PP Care*
Employer A		
Deductible	$200	Waived
Coinsurance	80%/20%	90%/10%
Employer B		
Deductible	$250	$200
Coinsurance	75%/25%	80%/20%
Employer C		
Deductible	$250	Waived
Coinsurance	75%/25%	90%/10%

Also, the out-of-pocket (OOP) maximum is often adjusted so that those employees who use nonpreferred providers do not reach the OOP maximum as quickly as those who use preferred providers. Therefore, the financial incentive to use preferred providers remains intact.

-239-

When incorporating a PPO into the health plan, what employee education is necessary?

Employers should provide their employees with written material that carefully explains the reasons for the PPO plan, identifies the preferred providers, and then explains the differences in reimbursement for preferred provider and nonpreferred provider care. Most employers find that continual written and visual communications are necessary. Employee meetings allow employees to ask questions and learn about the changes occurring in the health care delivery system.

-240-

Is an employer that elects a plan with a PPO sacrificing quality care for low cost?

Enough competition exists in many areas to encourage providers to lower their prices while continuing to provide high-quality care. The UR process helps ensure that this will continue. It is possible that the present competitive environment will *improve* the quality of care, rather than reduce it in many situations.

-241-

Can any employer include a PPO in its health care plan?

No. To date, formal PPOs have been developed only in areas where there is heavy competition among providers. Many rural areas with only a few physicians and one community hospital do not justify the work involved in establishing a PPO, although providers' practice patterns and costs may be a problem.

In addition, not all insurers offer PPOs. An insurer must have a significant market share in an area in order to justify the effort required to establish a PPO. Some insurers may have other health care delivery arrangements that offer employers similar cost-management techniques.

-242-

What other kinds of health care delivery arrangements are available to employers?

PPOs and HMOs represent integrations of services, but there are other arrangements as well. A catchall term for these arrangements is "vertical integration." In this case, integration combines all services under one umbrella in order to meet one need—health care. Suppliers, providers, and financers of services are now joining together in various ways to deliver health care, thereby creating opportunities for increased efficiency, improved services, and lower costs for health care consumers.

For example, insurers are acquiring HMOs and integrating them into their health care plans rather than having to compete with them. Third-party administrators—claims payment organizations—are joining forces with physicians to implement quasi-PPOs for certain large employers that need only claims administration and utilization review. Hospitals are acquiring insurance companies and equipment suppliers. Significant integration will continue.

-243-

Is the federal government following this trend toward integration?

Yes. As the insurer for Medicare, the federal government also needs to manage health care reimbursement. Rather than integrating services, the Health Care Financing Administration began implementing a prospective payment system (PPS) for Medicare in 1983. (Some state Medicaid administrations have also implemented prospective payment systems.) Hospitals can expect a fixed reimbursement for each patient discharged, based not on the number and kinds of services delivered, but on the diagnosis of the patient. As discussed earlier in this chapter, the retrospective reimbursement system encourages providers to deliver more care. In contrast, PPS eliminates the incentive for hospitals to deliver unnecessary care.

-244-

How are payments determined on the basis of diagnosis?

In 1975, Yale University introduced a system of diagnosis-related groups (DRGs) for 467 diagnoses. Initially, these DRGs were meant to be used as a management and planning tool for the health care system. But because of the need for cost management, the federal government decided to apply them to reimbursement definitions. Payment schedules for all DRGs were developed. Patients' conditions are translated to a DRG, and the allowable charge is determined based on the payment schedule.

-245-

Are all Medicare claims paid on a DRG basis?

Currently, only hospital care is paid on a DRG basis. There are, however, some hospitalizations that are given special consideration under the DRG system of reimbursement. These fall into two groups. First, certain kinds of hospitals are not required to subscribe to DRG rules to date. These include some teaching and psychiatric hospitals where the model for the determination of payment by diagnosis has not been developed yet, due to the different services involved and the complex issue of allowable costs of education involved at teaching hospitals. The other kinds of hospitalizations that are given special consideration are known as "outliers." Individuals whose illnesses are unique may not be classifiable under one of the DRGs. They may require care that is necessary but outside the realm of the established reimbursement norms. These cases are handled individually for Medicare reimbursement.

-246-

If the care delivered costs a hospital less than the DRG-allowed sum, does the hospital retain the difference as profit?

Yes. It is hoped that DRGs will encourage cost-effective care. Conversely, if the care provided costs the hospital more than it is reimbursed for under DRG, the hospital must make up the difference.

-247-

Are physicians reimbursed on a DRG basis?

Physicians are not yet being reimbursed on a DRG basis. The government has frozen reimbursement levels to physicians for their Medicare services since 1985. Studies are now being conducted to establish DRG reimbursement for physicians' services.

-248-

Are DRGs reducing the delivery of expensive, unnecessary hospital care?

There is some evidence that DRGs are having this effect. There are also arguments by health care professionals that patients have been discharged early, and without proper care, because their DRG wouldn't allow the hospital to continue care. Reconciliation of cost and quality of care under this system is still evolving.

-249-

Is Medicare the only plan that uses the DRG reimbursement system?

No. New Jersey law requires all reimbursement by insurers to be done on a DRG basis. There may also be other situations in which insurers have agreed to reimburse on a DRG basis through a private insurance arrangement at a particular hospital.

-250-

How has the DRG system affected the insurance industry?

DRGs have forced some hospitals to "cost shift" the revenue they lose from DRGs to other insurers. Many insurers—private companies, as well as state Medicaid administrations—are championing the introduction of "all payer" systems, under which all insurers would pay on the same basis, although not necessarily on a DRG basis. Some states—Maine, Maryland, Massachusetts, New Jersey, New York, and Washington—already have such a system in effect. In other states, the federal government has granted so-called Medicare waivers. These allow all insurers in these states to pay based on the prospective rating system rather than on the DRG system. These waivers are granted only in states where the costs to Medicare are expected to be lower than with DRG payment. The objective is to allow experimentation with other prospective payment systems that may eventually save money for our entire health care system.

Flexible Benefits

As the name denotes, flexible benefits plans come in all shapes to meet the needs of employees with diverse life styles and employers with varied objectives. This chapter covers the basic principles involved in the design and handling of flexible benefits plans, with emphasis on cafeteria plans as provided for under Section 125 of the Internal Revenue Code. These plans are new to the marketplace and promise to meet the needs of a changing work force, while providing a cost-management tool to employers.

-251-

What is a flexible benefits plan?

Flexible benefits plans are employee benefits plans based on the concept of employee choice. Traditional benefits plans offer each employee the same benefits and the same level of coverage, such as $50,000 of life insurance and a comprehensive medical plan with a $200 deductible and 80% coinsurance. Under a flexible benefits plan, employees have the opportunity to select individually the type of benefits and the level of coverage desired from those offered by their employers.

Flexible benefits is a generic name given to an employee benefits plan that offers employees a choice of benefits and coverage options. If the flex plan is designed in accordance with the tax provisions of Section 125 of the Internal Revenue Code, it is legally known as a cafeteria or Section 125 plan. Cafeteria plans allow an employee to choose between cash and several statutory nontaxable benefits, such as group life or medical insurance. It should be noted, however, that flexible plans can be developed independently of Section 125 plans. Plans developed independently of Section 125 are not in accordance with the tax provisions of the section and thus are restricted to offering choices only among nontaxable benefits, which excludes cash benefits. In this text, the term "flexible plan" refers to a plan that offers choices only among nontaxable benefits. The term "cafeteria plan" will refer to a plan that offers choices between cash *and* nontaxable benefits. The term "flexible benefits" will be used to describe the employee benefits choice phenomenon in general.

-252-

When were flexible benefits plans first introduced?

The first flexible benefits plans were established by large companies in the early 1970s. In 1978, the first legislation that specifically allowed cafeteria plans, the Revenue Act of 1978, was enacted. The Act added Section 125 to the Internal Revenue Code, under which a plan could legally offer a choice between nontaxable benefits and taxable benefits or cash without adverse tax consequences to employees.

Previously, the doctrine of "constructive receipt" served to limit the growth of flexible plans. Based on Section 2006 of the Employee Retirement Income Security Act (ERISA), the *right* to receive cash or other taxable benefits constituted constructive receipt even if the employee did not choose cash or a taxable benefit. Simply put, an employee could be taxed on benefits he or she never received if the employee merely had the right to choose them. As a result, ERISA effectively inhibited the development of flexible benefits plans by making all employer contributions to such plans taxable as ordinary income. The Revenue Act of 1978 provided an exception to the doctrine of constructive receipt.

While flexible benefits have been in existence for over 10 years, only recently have they been available to small and medium-sized employers. This was due to the fact that only large companies had the resources to implement and administer flexible benefits plans.

However, technological innovations have decreased the cost and have streamlined the process of administering the plans, and insurance companies have learned to adequately predict the cost and selection of the benefits offered under such plans. As a result, they are now available to companies with as few as 50 employees.

-253-

Why were flexible benefits plans developed?

Flexible benefits plans were developed as a result of two significant trends in the business world: a changing employee population with changing needs, and a need to control or manage escalating employee benefits costs.

In 1981, a survey of 1,000 corporations by the U.S. Chamber of Commerce revealed that their pension and benefits costs had tripled since 1971—to a staggering $485 billion annually. That same 10-year period saw inflation of 124% and wage increases of 115%. Since 1970, benefits costs as a percentage of payroll have nearly doubled—from 11.5% in 1970 to 19% in 1982.

The major component of these increases is the skyrocketing cost of health care. In 1950, health care costs were 4.4% of the GNP. By 1982, they had risen to 10.5%. By 1992, it's estimated that the U.S. will spend more than $1 trillion annually on health-related expenses.

The development of flexible benefits was also a response to a changing work force with varied needs. Traditional benefits plans were designed in the 1950s, when 60% of the work force consisted of men who were sole wage earners whose wives did not work. Today, however, this number has dropped to 34%. In fact, while only 30.5% of all wives worked in 1960, more than 50% were working by 1982. In addition to these changes, there are more women working than ever before; and there are more two-income families and single-parent families.

These demographic changes mean that a standard benefits package is inappropriate for the majority of today's workers. For example, a single person will not need or want as much life or health insurance as an older, married person with children. A single parent may need day care or more life insurance. An older worker with no children may need more medical but less life insurance. Thus, different life styles give rise to different benefits needs, and workers today are asking for benefits that are more meaningful to them.

-254-

How do flexible benefits help control costs?

The very structure of traditional benefits plans mandates cost increases each year. That's because medical care costs have increased each year, and at a rate faster than the consumer price index. A plan designed to cover the reasonable and customary charge for services, as most plans do, becomes more expensive as the cost of the services increases.

Flexible benefits provide a vehicle for separating the *level* of benefits from the *cost* of benefits. Employers can:

- Fix benefits costs as a percentage of payroll;
- Freeze costs at a set dollar level;
- Cover increased costs;
- Increase benefits as productivity or profits increase;
- Add new benefits without increasing the cost of the benefits program;
- Manage choices by controlling the price the employee pays for the benefits he or she selects; or
- Control the options employees can select through plan design.

An employer with a traditional plan has several options for controlling costs: limiting the coverage provided, increasing the extent to which employees pay for the services provided (through increased deductible and coinsurance requirements), and increasing employees' contributions to the plan, all of which create the impression that the employee is "giving back" benefits.

-255-

Are there different types of flexible plans?

Yes. There are three basic types of flexible plans:

(1) Total flexible benefits;
(2) Core plus; and
(3) Modular plans.

Total flexible plans provide employees with the greatest degree of choice and thus are most effective at meeting employee needs. Employees can select the appropriate level of coverage for each benefit offered through the plan. For example, they may be given three or four life insurance options, from which they can select one. Then they choose their medical coverage from several choices, and so on with disability, dental, and other insurance options that are provided.

Core plus flexible plans require a certain level of benefits for all employees participating in the benefits plan, with employees having the option to increase one or all of the coverages. The core level is usually funded by the employer. For example, with this plan, employees would be provided with $50,000 life insurance, a comprehensive medical plan with a $500 deductible, and disability insurance equal to 50% of salary. They would then have the option to increase their life, medical, or disability insurance benefits if they so desired, or perhaps add dental, which was not included in the core. These plans are more responsive to employee needs than modular plans, but considerably less responsive then total flexible benefits plans.

Modular flexible plans offer employees a choice of benefits packages. The employer determines combinations of coverages from which employees may choose. The employee selects the benefits package rather than choosing the level of coverage within each benefit. For example, Plan A might have life insurance equal to three times salary, a comprehensive medical plan with a $200 deductible and 80% coinsurance, and disability insurance equal to 50% of salary. Plan B might have life insurance equal to two times salary, a comprehensive medical plan with a $400 deductible and 80% coinsurance, and disability insurance equal to 60% of salary. Plan C might have life insurance equal to salary, a comprehensive medical plan with a $1,000 deductible and 80% coinsurance, and disability equal to 60% of salary. Each employee could then choose Plan A, B, or C, or, if the employer allows, none of the plans at all. Employees could not, however, choose only part of each plan. Generally, these plans are only partially responsive to employee needs.

-256-

What are the advantages of including a 401(k) plan in a flexible plan?

In addition to the tax advantages to both employers and employees, packaging with a flex plan makes administration of the 401(k) plan easier for the employer. The same salary reduction payroll system is used for both plans, and employees make their contribution and coverage choices at the same time. Also, employees may appreciate their benefits package more if they see the total package in an integrated manner.

-257-

What medical insurance options are available under a flexible plan?

The design of medical options under a flexible benefits plan is not restricted. However, offering a base plus plan as an option is not advisable if cost control is an objective. In fact, a flex plan provides an opportunity for an employer to move its plan from a base plus to a more cost-effective comprehensive plan, or to increase the deductible on a comprehensive plan, with less difficulty.

Most flexible plans offer several choices of deductibles and out-of-pocket maximums. Some include a catastrophe plan with a very high deductible and no coinsurance, and may allow an employee to take no medical coverage at all if he or she is covered elsewhere. The deductibles are designed with different life situations in mind and combined so that the choices among options are meaningful.

-258-

Can a flexible plan include an HMO?

Yes, an HMO can be among the medical options offered in a flexible plan. Evidence indicates that this adversely affects the cost of the rest of the plan, whether it is insured or self-funded, since younger, healthier employees are more likely to choose the HMO. However, if a qualified HMO has taken the required steps to initiate the offer, certain employers, as described at Questions 204 and 205, must offer that HMO.

-259-

Can a flex plan include a PPO?

Yes, a PPO can be incorporated into one or more of the medical options offered in a flexible plan. The level of reimbursement for each person will depend on whether the insured uses a preferred provider or not, as well as on the plan option selected for the plan year. The PPO arrangement is the same as it would be for a traditional plan.

-260-

Is all the insurance provided under a flexible plan provided by one insurer, or do insurers bid for pieces?

Plans may be designed and handled either way. However, small employers often prefer to place all coverage and reimbursement accounts with one insurer, since it simplifies implementation and administration.

-261-

What are the advantages of using one carrier?

When using one carrier, integration of all parts of the plan is inherent in its design, and all procedures, including enrollment, are coordinated. This makes installation more efficient. On an ongoing basis, plan administrators deal with one set of procedures, and forms and processes can be streamlined. For example, claims submitted but not covered in full under the medical or dental insurance plan can be automatically transferred for reimbursement from the health care reimbursement account. All of this should add up to lower costs in the long run.

-262-

Does a cafeteria plan allow employees to select cash instead of benefits?

Yes, although the degree to which employees can receive cash instead of benefits varies by employer. Some employers require that employees maintain a level of insurance protection (through their spouse's plan, for example) if the employee wishes to forgo all benefits and select cash exclusively.

-263-

What are the tax advantages of a cafeteria plan?

An employer's FICA and FUTA contributions are based on its payroll, and an employee's FICA contribution and local, state, and federal tax are based on gross income. Because employee contributions to cafeteria plans are on a pretax basis, they reduce the employer's payroll and the employee's taxable income by the amount of the contribution. Consequently, the employer's FICA and FUTA contributions decrease. The employee also benefits, because he or she is able to spend these benefit dollars and not pay taxes on them; therefore, employees get "more bang for their buck."

-264-

What types of benefits can cafeteria plans include?

Cafeteria plans can include the same statutory nontaxable benefits that traditional employee benefits plans do: life, medical, and dental insurance, and long- and short-term disability. They can also include such nontraditional features as a health care reimbursement account, a dependent care reimbursement account, a 401(k) plan, additional vacation days, and, if its nontaxable status continues, legal insurance.

-265-

What is a health care reimbursement account?

Health care reimbursement accounts, established under Section 105(h) of the Internal Revenue Code, allow participants to recover expenses on a pre-tax basis for those health care charges not reimbursed by any other source and not claimed on the participant's income tax return. These expenses can include, but are not limited to, medical and dental insurance deductibles and coinsurance; amounts over the reasonable and customary charges not covered by insurance; and other reimbursable expenses permitted as income tax deductions if medical expenses exceed 5% of gross income, such as contact lenses, orthopedic shoes, nursing, prescription drugs, lab tests, cosmetic surgery, hearing aids, etc.

-266-

What is a dependent care reimbursement account?

A dependent care reimbursement account allows for the use of pretax dollars to provide benefits for the care of (1) a dependent under the age of 15 for whom a dependent deduction is allowed under the Internal Revenue Code or (2) a dependent who is physically or mentally incapable of caring for him- or herself, to enable the benefits plan participant and his or her spouse to work. This benefit works in conjunction with the dependent care deduction available on the participant's income tax return; however, expenses reimbursed through this account may not be claimed for income tax purposes.

-267-

How are these accounts structured?

Health care and dependent care reimbursement accounts can be structured through a salary reduction agreement, employer contributions to the plan, or both. The employer sets the maximum amount of contribution allowed for each account at the beginning of the plan year. Each participant may choose to contribute an amount per plan year up to that maximum. The participant submits expenses to be reimbursed periodically from funds in his or her account. Reimbursement is permitted only for services provided during the plan year, and generally only up to the amount already accumulated in the individual's account from periodic deposits. Expenses in excess of the amount accumulated are held until funds are available.

-268-

What happens to any dollars accumulated but not used during the plan year?

Any dollars in an employee's account not used for services during the plan year are forfeited. Employees have some time after the end of the plan year to submit requests for reimbursement for services received during the plan year. Although their use is not specifically addressed in any law, there is some indication that these funds can be used by the employer to reduce costs in subsequent years, distributed on a per capita basis to employees who participated in the applicable account, or donated to a charitable organization.

-269-

Can a 401(k) plan be integrated into a cafeteria plan?

Yes. The Miscellaneous Revenue Act of 1980 amended Section

125 to allow cafeteria plans to include 401(k) plans, which are "cash-or-deferred" arrangements under which employers can make non-taxable contributions to qualified defined-contribution plans. Employees can make similar contributions through salary reduction, thereby deferring taxes on a portion of their incomes. 401(k) plans are the only deferred-compensation plans allowed in cafeteria plans. Contributions to 401(k) plans are subject to FICA taxes.

-270-

Why wouldn't all employees choose the plan options that offered the best coverage?

The benefits provided under each option in a cafeteria plan are often the same or similar. What differs is the level of coverage offered and the cost of the coverage. For example, an employee can choose one of several life insurance coverage levels—the difference is in the amount of insurance protection the employee elects. With medical coverage under a flexible plan, the deductibles and the out-of-pocket maximums generally are the differentiation factors, although the coinsurance level and benefit features may also vary, especially in a catastrophic option. While one choice may be "richer" than another, it will cost more. Many employees prefer not to pay this extra cost. They feel that these benefit dollars would be more wisely spent on another insurance coverage for which they have greater need, or they would prefer to receive the difference either in cash or as deposits to their 401(k) accounts.

-271-

What nondiscrimination requirements must a cafeteria plan meet to qualify under Section 125?

The Deficit Reduction Act of 1984 (DEFRA) added a new "top-heavy" rule that imposed additional requirements on cafeteria plans.

Under this rule, no more than 25% of the total nontaxable benefits may be provided to key employees. A key employee is:

- An officer earning more than $45,000;
- One of the ten employees owning the largest interest in the employer and earning more than $30,000 annually;
- A 5% owner; or
- A 1% owner earning more than $150,000 per year.

If the plan violates the top-heavy rule, the anti-constructive-receipt rule of Section 125 will not apply to *key* employees. They will be taxed as if they actually received all the taxable benefits that they could have elected to receive for the plan year.

-272-

How are plans tested to assure compliance with nondiscrimination rules?

Some nondiscrimination rules should be addressed at the plan design stage. These relate to such provisions as eligibility and equal benefits and contributions. Rules that cover participation and selection cannot be dealt with until all enrollment forms are completed. Then the insurer or administrator will test each part of the plan to be sure it is in compliance. Sometimes, changes must be made to bring the plan into compliance. For example, several highly compensated employees may be required to reduce their contributions to the health care reimbursement account.

Although nondiscrimination rules are still in the process of being clarified and refined, every effort must be made to interpret and apply current rules consistently.

-273-

How are flexible benefits plans funded?

Typically, flexible benefits plans are funded in three ways: employer contributions to the plan, employee contributions to the plan through a salary reduction agreement, or both. The way in which flexible benefits plans are funded does not differ from the funding of traditional employee benefits plans, with one notable exception: Employee contributions to the plan are on a pretax basis (see Question 256).

-274-

Must flexible benefits plans be contributory?

Any one of the options under each coverage may be fully funded by the employer either for the employee only or for family coverage, making it "noncontributory" in the traditional sense. However, other options under that coverage may require employee contributions. Thus, the plan as a whole could be looked at as "contributory." This does not preclude the possibility that given the employer's funding, an individual employee could select coverages and levels in each that would be fully noncontributory.

-275-

How does an employer determine its level of contribution to the plan?

There are a number of ways for employers to determine their levels of contribution to a flexible plan, such as freezing benefits costs as a percentage of payroll, determining a set dollar amount they wish to spend on employee benefits, or contributing the same amount they did under the traditional benefits plan. All of these options, however, are based on the employer's objectives in establishing a flexible plan. While these objectives may differ for each employer, they can generally be broken down into three categories, which are not necessarily exclusive:

(1) To attract and retain the best employees;
(2) To control costs; or
(3) To reduce costs while maintaining an adequate benefits plan.

The contribution level will differ, just as the structure and design of the plan will vary according to the employer's objectives. If the plan is a tool to attract and retain employees, employer contributions would probably be higher than if the objective is to reduce costs.

-276-

How are employee contribution levels determined?

Employee contributions are determined by the employer at the beginning of each plan year and vary depending on a number of factors, including the cost of the plan, the benefits each employee selects, and the level of employer contributions.

-277-

How are employer and employee contributions made in a flexible benefits plan?

Employer contributions are commonly made by allocating credits to a "decision pool." Employee contributions consist of pretax contributions to the decision pool. A decision pool represents the combined contributions of employer and employee, and is the amount available for each employee to pay insurance premiums for chosen benefits, fund reimbursement accounts, or receive as cash in lieu of benefits.

-278-

Can small employers self-fund flexible benefits plans?

Small employers can self-fund their flexible benefits plans, but the adverse selection issues discussed in Question 280 become more acute for them. If self-funding is desired, employers need a skilled and experienced intermediary to assist with plan design, implementation, administration, and renewal. Since flex is in the early stages of development, few intermediaries have this expertise.

-279-

Is purchasing a flexible benefits plan similar to purchasing a traditional one?

Flexible benefits plans are purchased in much the same way that traditional plans are. The employer, working with its insurance intermediary (broker, agent, or consultant), might survey employees to determine their needs, and must establish the employer's objectives. The intermediary then solicits quotes from insurers and selects the desired benefits provider based on those needs and objectives.

-280-

Does an employer need an insurer to implement a flexible benefits plan?

For an employer with fewer than 500 employees that is implementing a flexible benefits plan for the first time, an insurer is highly recommended. This is because the financial risk associated with benefits utilization in a flexible benefits plan is greater than with a traditional benefits plan.

Traditional benefits plan premium rates are calculated to reflect the average use of benefits by a diverse group of employees. Some employees will use some benefits—for example, medical or disability benefits—and others will not use any at all. Because of this, the premiums for employees who do not use any benefits help pay for the benefits that are used.

However, with a flexible benefits plan, employees select a package of benefits that reflects their specific needs. Thus, they are most likely to select benefits they will actually use. For example, healthy employees and dependents are more likely to buy higher-deductible medical plans at lower cost. This phenomenon is known as "adverse selection." Adverse selection does not actually cause higher utilization of benefits, because employees generally use what they need, and claims remain the same. What does result is less premium being available from those who don't use their benefits to pay for benefits that are used.

This means, then, that pricing the benefits in a flexible benefits plan and predicting benefits utilization is a complicated process. Insurance companies and the larger consulting firms have actuarial professionals who can estimate fairly accurately the expected cost of each flexible benefits plan component, and can make demographic predictions of who will elect certain benefits as well as who will use the benefits. In addition, the financial resources of most insurers allow them to absorb the financial consequences of some inaccurate predictions. In the future, as the accuracy of prediction of utilization increases, employers may be in a better position to consider assuming more of the risk of flexible benefits plans. Small employers will still be subject to the volatility of utilization that comes with being able to spread the risk over only a relatively few employees.

-281-

What specific issues should an employer address in contemplating the purchase of a flexible benefits plan?

Most companies adopt flexible benefits plans to meet the needs of a diverse work force, to attract and retain employees, to manage and control costs, and to achieve tax-effective use of their benefits dollars. However, while these are the basic reasons for purchasing a flexible plan, designing a plan to meet these objectives requires a more precise analysis.

The specific issues that employers should address before designing a plan include whether the company is interested in:

- Offering better benefits than companies competing with it for skilled labor;
- Raising employee morale by offering better benefits;
- Retaining top-level management;
- Preventing unionization;
- Improving the company's image;
- Increasing equity in benefits among employees, regardless of marital status or income;

- Increasing employees' awareness of the cost of medical care;
- Separating benefits costs from benefits levels; or
- Spending no more than a set dollar amount on the benefits package for a fixed period of time.

Plan features, including coverages, levels, and costs, can be designed differently to accomplish the objectives of each individual company. For example, if a company wants to offer a more attractive benefits plan than its competition, but still needs to control costs, the flexible plan can be designed so that the employer provides the same level of benefits as under its traditional plan, but gives employees the option to purchase additional benefits through pretax salary reduction. For an employer that is interested in cost control and therefore determines that it cannot spend more than a set dollar amount on benefits for a fixed period of time, the plan can be structured so that the benefits offered remain the same, and the employer's contribution remains the same even if the cost of benefits rises. In such an example, the employee would assume more responsibility for the purchase of the benefits if he or she wanted to maintain the previous level of benefits.

Thus, while there are certain basic criteria for adopting a plan, properly designing one requires an analysis of that specific company's situation, the employer's objectives, and the employees' benefits needs.

-282-

How can an employer determine what its employees' benefits needs are?

Employee needs can be determined by a written survey that should be administered at least six months before the proposed effective date of the flexible benefits plan. When planned and analyzed carefully by the employer, consultant, or insurer, a survey can provide valuable information for designing a flexible plan that will be well-received by employees. Just as employers must determine precisely what their needs are, it is important to determine what employees want in their benefits package.

In addition, an employee-needs survey is one tool for having the employees participate in designing the plan. This involvement, in turn, will lead to greater employee acceptance of the flexible plan and the advantages it offers. However, some employers feel a survey is unnecessary. They have other reliable means of knowing their employees' needs and would prefer not to spend the time to conduct a survey.

-283-

How are flexible benefits plans implemented?

Implementing a flexible benefits plan is generally the same as for a traditional plan: The plan is announced, employees are enrolled and receive information concerning their benefits coverages, and the plan then becomes effective. However, while the basic outline for plan implementation remains the same, each of the steps involved requires different tactics. For example, the plan announcement requires more communication from the company to the employees in order to explain the new concept of flexible benefits, and the enrollment of employees is more involved.

-284-

How long does it take from the purchase of a flexible benefits plan until it can be implemented?

The preliminary analysis of employer objectives and employee needs can take somewhat longer than for a traditional benefits plan, depending on the size of the employer and the complexities involved in compensation analysis. This analysis will be done before the plan is quoted, as with traditional plans.

The time from the initial quote on the plan design to the actual effective date of the plan is usually at least four months. The first month is spent reviewing the quote for its success in meeting the employer's determined objectives. Actual implementation, once the decision to buy has been made and the final plan design settled on, requires two and a half to three months.

-285-

What kinds of employee communications are advisable in advance of enrollment?

As the size of the employee group increases, so does the intensity of the communications effort involved in flexible benefits plan implementation. Regardless of size, however, careful, clear communication is essential. Employers usually use a letter from the chief executive officer or president of the company to announce the flexible benefits plan. Posters may be placed in strategic locations around the company to introduce the concept of flex. Also, in preparation for enrollment, some explanation of the concept of flexible benefits, in easily understood form, should be given to employees. A simple conceptual brochure can serve this purpose.

-286-

How do employees enroll in a plan and select their benefits?

Since understanding is so critical to making the most appropriate choices, employee meetings are usually held to explain the flexible benefits plan. They may be conducted by the employer, an intermediary, the insurer, or a combination of them. At those meetings, employees are provided with a written explanation of the process and forms on which to make their selections. The forms will typically identify the benefits options and their costs, as well as the amount of benefits dollars provided by the employer. Employees are expected to make choices and calculate their total costs including the salary reduction that will result if selections cost more than the amount the employer provides. If an employee opts for fewer benefits than his or her benefits dollars cover, the plan might provide that he or she receive the excess as additional taxable income.

To minimize confusion to employees, particularly during the first plan year, enrollment requires a great deal of employee education, even after employee meetings have been held and the materials have been distributed. An employer representative must be knowledgeable and should be available to answer questions during the enrollment period, which is usually at least two months prior to the effective date. This educational effort takes time, but the employer's genuine concern for employee needs is communicated repeatedly, often resulting in increased employee morale.

The enrollment process can result in some dissatisfied employees, especially if previous benefits were extremely comprehensive and some new limitations are being imposed. It is advisable for management to determine what communication of compensation objectives is necessary before the flexible benefits plans is announced, to assure maximum satisfaction.

-287-

What is enrollment confirmation?

Employees are provided with a summary of their individual benefits choices and the costs associated with them. They are asked to verify the accuracy of the summary by signing and returning it to the company's personnel accounting department, which in turn directs it to the administrator of the flexible plan. Usually a short period is allowed for employees to change their choices or correct any errors or misunderstandings. Once signed, the summary serves as confirmation that the employee's choices are correct as recorded, and benefits will be paid based on the record.

-288-

What kinds of changes may an employee make during the plan year?

Tax law requires that an employee's choices in a flexible benefits plan be made in advance of the plan year. This means that after the effective date of the plan, no changes can be made (except as described below) until the next enrollment period. Changes in choices during the plan year are permitted only if a "family status" change occurs. A family status change is defined to include changes such as the following:

- Marriage;
- Divorce;
- Death of a spouse;
- Birth of a child;
- Adoption of a child; or
- Termination of employment of a spouse.

-289-

How do the cost and pricing of a flexible benefits plan compare with those of a traditional employee benefits plan?

The cost issue has two parts: (1) the cost of the benefits themselves, which incorporates the risk of adverse selection and the potential for cost management inherent in a flexible benefits plan; and (2) the cost involved in developing and implementing the program.

The cost of the benefits, if insured, will be based on the insurer's underlying price structure, which usually applies to traditional as well as flexible benefits plans. Traditional insurance allows insurers to calculate an average rate for the group to be covered and multiply it by the number of employees and dependents enrolled or, for some coverages, by the volume of insurance elected overall. Insurers' methods for flexible plan pricing vary. They must take into account selection assumptions and utilization rates that vary accordingly. The risk of selection is in addition to the utilization risks in a single traditional plan. It may be assumed by the employer or the insurer. An intermediary can help the employer obtain an acceptable pricing agreement with an insurer.

Cost management or control is most applicable to medical coverage. Decisions about features like coinsurance variations, deductibles, and preferred provider arrangements are not inherently different for flexible benefits plan coverages, but a flexible plan, by virtue of the availability of choice, allows an employer to introduce plan features that promise long-term cost control. Furthermore, by establishing the basis for the future contributions for the employee benefits plan, an employer can begin the process of long-term cost management.

Depending on who performs the services associated with design and implementation of the plan, the costs of these services may be charged separately or incorporated in the benefits cost. Excellent communications materials and enrollment assistance are available to employers of all sizes at reasonable costs. Ongoing administration costs generally depend on the frequency of the services requested, such as reimbursement account payments and reports.

-290-

How does renewal of a flexible benefits plan compare with traditional employee benefits plan renewal?

Annual reenrollment makes renewal of a flexible benefits plan somewhat more time-consuming. Renewal costs will be based on prior elections and anticipated changes, plan design adjustments, and the insurer's medical care costs in general, as well as, for some plans, the past experience of the total plan and its options separately. The process also takes more time than for traditional plans, since there are more alternatives for meeting the employer's objectives, which also may have changed.

-291-

What kinds of reports are necessary to ensure smooth implementation and administration of the plan?

In addition to the standard reports associated with benefits utilization, additions and deletions of employees and dependents, and premium accounting reports, three flexible benefits plan reports are necessary. A salary impact report is usually generated after enrollment confirmation. This identifies the costs of the benefits and the salary reduction or increase associated with each employee's choices. It is the blueprint for changes to the employer's payroll system.

For plans with health care reimbursement or dependent care reimbursement accounts, periodic reports are necessary for employees and the employer to summarize available funds in each account and payments made from them. For plans with 401(k) plans, an individual periodic report showing employee contributions, employer contributions, interest, and fund balances is recommended, as well as an employer summary for the plan.

-292-

How does an employer decide who will administer the flexible benefits plan?

After understanding what is involved in administering a flexible benefits plan, an employer must evaluate the options available. Resources (both systems and people), priorities, and cost should be considered, taking into account the efficiencies of working with one source for the entire plan.

The employer may decide for simplicity's sake to select an insurer that has the ability to administer the plan as well as provide the plan design and coverage options. Insurers that do offer flexible plans to small employers will generally also offer administrative support. Some insurers also offer special software packages to small employers for plan administration.

If the employer has the systems necessary to administer the plan or is willing to invest in such areas because of anticipated cost savings, then the employer could administer the plan itself. Third-party administrators are also an option, as are brokers and consultants who have the systems available. Thus, many options are available to the employer for administering the plan.

-293-

What type of billing arrangement is used—self-accounting or home office?

Complete records of each employee's current choices must be kept, regardless of how a flexible benefits plan is billed. Generally, the first bill would identify each employee and the costs associated with his or her selections. Subsequent bills can reflect only the changes to choices as a result of the addition of new employees, termination of employees, or changes in family status. This is somewhere between what is commonly referred to as self-accounting and home-office billing by insurance companies.

-294-

Will future legislation affect flexible benefits plans?

Future legislation will certainly affect the design of flexible benefits plans, primarily in terms of antidiscrimination rules and tax status of cafeteria plans. Changes in tax status, however, should have a relatively minor effect, since the real issue driving the growth of flexible benefits plans is long-term cost control and the desire by employees for choice in the benefits selection process. The importance of these elements in the development of flex is demonstrated by the growth of such plans among large and small employers since the early 1970s, a time of legislative uncertainty.

Plan Rating and Funding

Plan rating and funding are important aspects of group health insurance. The approach used is the basis on which the cost of the plan to the employer is determined. This chapter covers plan rating and funding techniques, including conventional funding, high self-insured plans, deferred premium, retrospective premium arrangements, reserve reduction arrangements, minimum premium, pooling, experience rating, stop-loss insurance, and self-funding.

-295-

What does plan funding mean?

Plan funding refers to the way claims liabilities will be financed. The fully insured insurance contract represents the most common method of financing claims: The policyholder pays a monthly premium, and the insurance company is liable for administering and paying claims for covered expenses. For most small employers, this conventional funding is the most appropriate approach to fund the costs of a health care plan.

-296-

What are the components of the cost of a health insurance plan?

No matter what funding vehicle is used, the cost components of a plan are similar. They are:

- Expected claims;
- Margin for higher claims than expected;
- Reserves for future claims;
- Expenses; and
- The insurer's profit charge.

-297-

What are expected claims?

The amount of claims that will be incurred during the policy year is estimated by the insurer. The estimate includes claims payments that are expected to be made during that policy year as well as claims payments for expenses incurred during that year, but not reported until after the end of the year. Thus, expected claims are composed of:

- Claims expected to be reported and paid in the policy year;
- Claims incurred during the year but not paid in that year; and
- Claims for which the insurer is liable after the contract terminates.

While payments that will be made after termination of the contract for claims are also typically included in this "expected claims" projection, exactly what claims an insurer is liable for varies from contract to contract.

-298-

Why would claims be paid after the termination of the contract?

The insurer usually guarantees certain benefits after the termination of an insurance contract. For example, consider a situation in which an expense was incurred in April, but the claim was not submitted to the insurer until May; the employer has terminated coverage with the insurer as of April 30. The insurer is typically liable for paying the claim, since the expense was incurred while the coverage was in force, even if the employer has signed a contract with a new insurance company. In addition, under most policies the insurer is liable for "extended benefits" for employees who are disabled when an insurance contract terminates. Policies vary, but these benefits often cover expenses for a year after termination.

-299-

How does an insurer know what claims to expect?

Insurance actuaries base expected claims estimates on their past experience with large numbers of insureds, as well as on published statistical information regarding (1) the probability that individuals will incur medical expenses, (2) the plan design (what expenses are covered), and (3) the probable cost of those expenses. Deviations between "expected" and "actual" claims are very common on a policy-by-policy basis. An insurer hopes to accurately estimate expected claims for its entire block of business, thus collecting enough premium to pay claims overall.

-300-

What is a group health insurance actuary?

A group health insurance actuary is an accredited insurance mathematician who analyzes health care providers' costs associated with delivering health care and insurance companies' costs associated with insuring against the risk of incurring health care expenses. Traditionally, actuaries have focused on group morbidity and mortality and insurance administrative expenses to develop premium rate structures for health coverage.

As the health care delivery system has changed and expanded, the cost of health care and health care insurance has increased dramatically. As a result, actuaries have put increased emphasis on analyzing costs of health care providers, and have used these data—along with more traditional data—as the basis for determining the rate structures of insurance carriers. The premium rate structure is the basis for determining the cost of coverage to each policyholder.

Prices vary according to the composition of the group and the health benefit plan selected.

-301-

How does an actuary estimate which individuals will incur claims?

Actuarial data that reflect claims probabilities for individuals and groups of individuals according to certain characteristics are continuously compiled and updated. These data are available to actuaries through various insurance industry channels. The probability of incurring a medical expense is based primarily on age and sex, but some actuaries also consider the effects of income and occupation or industry.

For example, monthly expected claims for an architectural firm where the average age is 35 and 80% of the employees are male would usually be lower than for a retail store where the average age is 45 and the only 40% of the employees are male. This is because younger people are generally healthier, and women generally incur more claims than men, especially during their childbearing years. The claims for a group of highly paid professionals may be lower than for a group of lower-paid employees. In addition, actuarial statistics show that the incidence of claims is often higher for employees who are likely to change jobs frequently because they use their health care coverage when they have it, for fear that they may not have it at some point in the near future. Because better health is generally tied to higher socioeconomic status, all else being equal, insurers expect fewer claims from professionals, as compared with other employees.

-302-

How does plan design affect the expected claims calculation?

If the plan is a base plus major medical plan, claims will be higher, due to a reimbursement system that not only increases actual dollars for each hospital stay but also promotes expensive inpatient care. The absence of a deductible and coinsurance on the basic plan also leads to higher claims expenses for the insurer, since many small claims are submitted. (Premiums are higher by approximately 8% to 15% for base plus plans, as compared with comprehensive plans.)

For any plan, the amount of the deductible and coinsurance are the key factors that determine the cost. Today, many plans cover similar expenses, but the cost-sharing provisions vary. A comprehensive plan with a $300 individual annual deductible and a $1,000 out-of-pocket (OOP) maximum may cost approximately 6% less than a plan with a $100 deductible and a $500 OOP maximum. If the employer decides to include utilization review in the plan, hospital admissions and lengths of stay are expected to be lower than for a plan without this cost-management feature. Other cost-controlling features are discussed in the chapter entitled "Managing Health Insurance Costs."

-303-

How does the health plan's rate-guarantee period affect the rate?

Monthly premium rates are guaranteed to remain fixed for a specified period, such as one year. The longer the rate guarantee, the higher the rate. This is because of the difficulty of projecting the cost of health care in the future and the expectation that health care costs will continue to rise at least as fast as the consumer price index.

-304-

How does the insurer project the cost of the medical services that are expected?

The two components of claims cost projections are (1) geographic location and (2) medical care inflationary trends. Health care costs more, as do other goods and services, in certain areas of the country. In 1985, average hospital room and board in New York City was $435 per day, while in Bangor, Maine, the average cost was $230. Physicians' charges follow the same pattern. However, this situation is changing with the increase in competition for market share, especially in urban areas where there are many hospitals and thousands of physicians.

As PPOs and other integrated medical care and financing arrangements expand, actuaries will not be able to project costs based only on historical rates in certain geographic locations. As insurers make arrangements with providers, the pricing structure of medical care will often require actuaries to make entirely new calculations.

Medical care inflationary trends are also changing as broad realignments occur in the medical care delivery system. Historically, "trend" has been a component of every insurer's rate structure. It is a measure of the annual inflation rate of medical care goods and services and the effects of increased technology and utilization of services. Medical care costs have been rising much faster than the costs of other items; the trend component of most insurers' rates in 1982 was about 16%. That is, the insurer estimated that prices would rise during the year the contract was effective; thus, the rates were set initially at a point to cover those expected increases.

-305-

How is the expected cost of claims calculated for an employer with several locations?

The costs in each location are analyzed to develop claims. If there are large numbers of employees in more than one location, there may be separate rates for each location.

-306-

How is a margin for higher than anticipated claims developed?

Insurance company actuaries project how much fluctuation is

likely in their expected claims estimates, based on their experience with rate setting and the volatility of the medical care climate at the time a group rate is set. The margin that is added to the expected claims figure is based on the probable stability of the group, which varies with the size of the group and, for larger groups, is based on the past experience of the group.

-307-

What are reserves?

In broad terms, reserves are a measure of an insurance company's liability for future claims. Insurers establish a dollar amount for each group they insure that is an estimation of the amount of money they will need to fund claims payments for which they may be liable after policy termination. This reserve estimate is added to the claims estimate developed for the claims incurred in the present plan year to get an "expected claims" projection for a group.

-308-

How are expenses projected?

The expense components of premium include:

- The insurer's initial underwriting work;
- Issue of the contract and the plan materials, such as employee booklets;
- Ongoing plan administration (e.g., billing, the cost of paying claims, and underwriting work for plan changes and renewals);
- Premium taxes;
- Broker and agent commissions; and
- Contribution to the insurance company's overhead.

For small employers, average expenses are used, but for large employers, expenses are often itemized. For example, a charge for each claim paid could be agreed to by the policyholder and the insurer at the beginning of the plan year.

-309-

What percentage of the health care premium is generally an insurance company's profit?

Profit charges, like expense charges and methods for calculating expected claims, vary by insurer.

-310-

What is a manual rate?

A manual rate is the rate generally charged to groups with too few employees to create credible claims experience. It is a combination of the expected claims factor, the margin for higher than anticipated claims, expenses, and profit. All four components are based on actuarial manual formulas that produce an approximation of expected "average" claims and "average" expenses, given the size of the employer and therefore the administration required. Manual rates are occasionally referred to as "pooled rates."

-311-

What is a pool?

When the term "pool" is used in the context of small policies, it refers to a large number of such policies that the insurer analyzes as a group. Claims projections for the group of policies can be more accurately estimated than for small policies individually—thus, the term "pooled rates." (See also Question 315.)

-312-

What is an experience rate?

An experience rate is a combination of the employer's specific expected claims estimation, a margin for higher than anticipated claims, expenses, and profit. For large employers (more than 500 employees), the margin, expenses, and profit are negotiated annually with the insurer.

If the group is large enough—generally more than 50 employees—the insurer will use past claims experience to project future claims experience. However, for groups with fewer than 200 employees, the insurer will not put full credibility in the past claims history to project the future.

Small employers thus have rates that are at least partially "manual." Larger employers have rates that are based partially on experience and are partially manual. Employers with several hundred employees are typically fully experience rated.

-313-

What is credibility?

Credibility refers to belief in the past claims experience as an indication of future claims experience. Each insurer interprets claims history differently, and each has a certain credibility formula that applies to groups that are large enough to be experience rated. The basis for the formula is the size of the employer in terms of both covered employees and annual premium or claims.

For example, an employer with 100 covered employees and an annual premium of $170,000 might be assigned a credibility factor of 50%. The insurer would develop an experience rate for the group, based on an analysis of the prior two or three years of claims history, and this rate would be 50% believable, or "credible."

-314-

How is an experience rate combined with a manual rate to produce a final premium rate?

For a case that is 50% credible, half of the experience rate and half of the manual rate would combine to form the final rate.

-315-

Do all claims count toward an employer's claims experience, thus affecting the rate?

Arrangements are usually made for insurers to "pool" claims over a certain dollar limit so that large, infrequent claims don't adversely affect the employer's claims/loss ratio. The employer pays a premium to the insurer for this protection, which keeps large claims amounts out of the experience rate analysis, so that the employer's rates won't increase as a result of occasional unpredictable claims.

-316-

What is a pool charge?

Some risks are excluded from an employer's experience, such as very large claims that are "pooled" rather than counted into the employer's claims experience for rate setting. The fee for this protection is called a pool charge.

Pool charges are included in the premium for all size cases, but for large cases, this premium is explicitly itemized as such. Small cases include premium for the risk of large claims, but for small policies, this is set by the actuary and is not negotiable. Larger employers, on the other hand, may choose to pool claims at a certain dollar level, based on the risk the employer wants to assume. Claims included in an employer's experience analysis will cause rates to fluctuate. The large employer must decide whether it is a better financial decision to pay a larger pool charge to be protected against claims, or to pay a smaller pool charge but be less protected from large claims risk.

-317-

What is a shock claim?

Shock claims, sometimes called "random claims," are large claims (over $10,000 at least, depending on the amount of the policy premium overall) usually resulting from an accident or severe illness of an individual.

-318-

What is retention?

An insurance company's retention is the premium charged for expenses and profit. Retention is generally an average charge for small employers, based on how much administration is typically required, the risk assumption involved, and the insurance company's profit margin. It is expressed as a percentage of premium. For small policies, the term "retention" is not generally used to refer to expenses and profit.

For larger employers or for policies that have alternative funding arrangements (see Questions 327–330), the term "retention" is used, and is usually a negotiated percentage of premium, ranging from 6% to 20%, based on the services and risk assumption the employer requires from the insurer.

-319-

How does an employer determine whether a premium rate is reasonable?

It is difficult for employers to determine the reasonableness of rates because it is difficult to make "apples to apples" comparisons among various plan quotes by insurance companies. Coverage provisions vary among insurers.

For employers whose rates are manual, the intermediary typically offers "spreadsheet" quotes from several carriers. Rate comparisons can be made, but differences in benefits must be carefully reviewed. Rate alone is not a good basis for choosing a plan.

For employers whose rates are partially or fully experience rated, the intermediary obtains quotes from several insurers, but because the quotes are based on more subjective information, which each insurer analyzes somewhat differently, there will be more rate negotiation than on smaller policies. One significant variation is in the amount of "credibility" the insurer assigns to a particular employer's past claims experience.

-320-

Are dependent rates developed separately from employee rates?

No. For manually rated employers and for larger employers with premium rates that are at least partially manual, dependent rates are derived from employee rates. Usually, spouses' actual ages are not required; the assumption is made that spouses' ages will average out to be the same as employees' ages. For the experience portion of a premium rate, the employer's loss ratio is reviewed as a whole, rather than by employee and dependent. Thus, even if only dependent claims were resulting in high loss ratios, employee rates as well as dependent rates would reflect these high losses. Rates quoted to the employer are separate, however. Usually, all premiums, both employee and dependent, are combined, as are claims.

-321-

What is a loss ratio?

An employer's loss ratio is an expression of claims compared with premium. A low ratio indicates "good" claims experience—the premium collected was more than required to fund the actual claims. A high loss ratio indicates that claims exceeded premium.

-322-

What is a tolerable loss ratio?

A tolerable loss ratio (TLR) is the loss ratio the insurer can fund without losing money on the group. The insurer projects what claims are expected for a certain group. Premium rates are set based on that projection of claims, plus the charges necessary to cover the insurer's expenses. A typical small employer's premium might be 82% for expected claims payments, and 18% for expenses—underwriting, issue, administration, claims processing, commissions, overhead, and profit.

The amount of claims that is "tolerable" in this case would be 82% of premium. The TLR would be 82%. A loss ratio of over 82% for this employer group indicates that the insurer did not accurately project claims.

The insurer has a TLR for its block of cases as a whole, as well as a target TLR for each policy. If the overall loss ratio exceeds the TLR, profits may be reduced or eliminated. In a year in which this occurred, the insurer would be forced to use previously acquired surplus to fund certain expenses.

-323-

Do TLRs vary from year to year and from employer to employer?

TLRs vary annually because expected claims and expenses vary from year to year. Expenses vary with the size of a group and with the plan design elected by the employer. Expected claims vary by group and plan design, and they also vary considerably from the first year of coverage to later years.

For the first year in which an insurance company underwrites an employee group, the claims actually *paid* are expected to be less than 80% of premium. Typically, first-year paid claims are estimated to be between 45% and 60% of premium. This is because claims that were incurred in the prior year under another insurance contract are usually paid by the prior insurer. That insurance company is liable for those "incurred but not reported" (IBNR) claims, not the present insurer. Employees are typically allowed to submit bills for expenses they incurred prior to master contract termination after that contract terminates.

The premiums charged by the new insurance company appear, at first glance, to be much too high, based on the expected paid claims for that first year the contract is in force. However, since the new insurer will be liable for claims *incurred* during the period the insurance contract is in force, even though they may not be reported and paid until later, it is necessary for it to collect premiums to fund the claims that will be paid at a later date. These premiums are known as "reserves."

-324-

What is the difference between *paid* claims and *incurred* claims?

Paid claims are claims actually paid in a defined period. Incurred claims are a combination of claims that are actually paid (checks sent to reimburse the expenses of insureds), claims that have occurred but have not been submitted for payment to date, and claims for which an insurer will be liable after termination of the contract. When an insurer develops a premium rate, incurred claims are used to set the rates, since the incurred claim estimate represents the insurer's total liability.

-325-

How does an insurer determine what premium reserves are necessary?

Insurance company actuaries develop projections of what the future claims liability will be for their entire pool of insured groups. They base their projections on the past experience of similar groups, and they factor in the expected cost increases of medical care and expected changes in utilization.

For smaller employers, an average percentage of premiums is usually used to develop the expected incurred claims estimate to set the premium rates. For instance, a certain employer with 50 employees might be expected to accumulate $54,000 of paid claims in the coming year and to submit claims for a total of $18,000 after the end of the year. This $18,000 represents expected claims to be incurred but not reported in the policy period—in this case, a year. The $18,000 projection would have been developed because this insurer projected a liability of approximately 26% of premium to surface after the first policy-year period, usually in bits and pieces over the subsequent three to six months.

The insurance company underwriting a new contract on a larger employer typically reviews the "run-out" claims of prior years to get an idea of the reserves that should be established for future liability. As a result of claims run-outs, "lag studies" are generated for underwriters to analyze.

-326-

What is a lag study?

A lag study is an analysis of the historical timing patterns of claims submissions. The results are used to estimate claims expected to be submitted after the end of the policy period. This helps the underwriter determine required reserves for the policy.

Lag studies are rarely done for employers with fewer than 300 employees, because of the high volume of claims necessary to make the studies believable projections. However, actuaries compile run-out patterns into lag studies for their *entire case block* to establish reserve requirements for the expected total run-out liability on their entire block of business.

-327-

Are there alternatives to fully insured (conventionally funded) plans?

Alternative funding vehicles allow the employer to absorb some of the risk that the insurer standardly assumes under a conventionally funded insurance plan. The alternatives include:

- Deferred premium (extended grace period);
- High self-insured deductibles (HSIDs);
- Retrospective premium arrangements;
- Reserve reduction agreements;
- Minimum premium plans (MPPs); and
- Administrative services only (ASO) plans.

Employers that elect alternative funding can be either partially self-funded or fully self-funded.

-328-

How do alternative funding methods differ from conventional methods of funding?

The fundamental differences are the split of risk between insurer and policyholder and the expenses associated with the alternative funding arrangement. The split of risk changes the insurer's liability for claims during the plan year as well as after contract termination. For example, the employer may elect to be responsible for funding individual conversions. By assuming additional risk, the employer can reduce its premium to the insurer. Expenses payable to the insurer vary, depending on what risks and services the insurer retains responsibility for. For instance, premium taxes are reduced to the extent premium is reduced when the employer assumes more risk.

-329-

For whom might an alternative to conventional plan funding be appropriate?

The rising cost of health care has resulted in increased interest in funding alternatives by many employers that want to:

- Improve their cash flow;
- Reduce premium taxes and insurance company charges; or

• Eliminate or reduce services provided in conventionally insured plans.

The way an employer can achieve any of these objectives is to assume some of the risk the insurer traditionally assumes. Whether a particular employer should attempt to do this depends on the size of the employer, the past claims experience of the group, the current health status of the employees, the risk attitude of the employer, and the willingness of an insurer to provide the employer with protection against whatever share of the risk the employer is unwilling to assume.

-330-

What size employers typically seek funding alternatives?

The majority of employers with fewer than 300 employees probably do *not* elect an alternative funding arrangement; however, employers with as few as 100 covered employees are sometimes candidates for nonconventional funding. Some insurers have special funding products for employers with as few as 50 employees.

Employers with fewer than 500 employees rarely fully self-fund. Even those that do almost always have stop-loss insurance as protection against excessive claims, such as individual claims for more than $50,000 or aggregate claims during a year for more than 25% of the employer's expected claims level.

-331-

What is stop-loss insurance?

Employers that partially or fully self-fund usually purchase stop-loss insurance to avoid large losses. The coverage reimburses the employer for claims that exceed a certain limit. Two types of stop-loss insurance are available: specific and aggregate.

-332-

What is the difference between aggregate and specific stop-loss insurance?

Specific stop-loss insurance limits the employer's liability to a predetermined amount for any single insured during a certain time period. For example, the specific stop-loss level might be set at $50,000 per insured per policy year. Typically, claims are determined on a paid, rather than incurred, basis. That is, claims actually paid during the policy year will count toward the stop-loss maximum for that year, and will not be carried over into subsequent policy years.

Aggregate stop-loss insurance limits the employer's liability to a predetermined amount for the entire insured group during a certain time period. For example, the aggregate stop-loss limit might be set at 125% of expected claims.

Employers may purchase both specific and aggregate stop-loss insurance, providing two ways of limiting or reducing an employer's insurance liability.

-333-

From whom does an employer purchase stop-loss insurance?

Most often, the employer arranges a stop-loss contract with the insurer that is involved in the rest of the plan. For example, if an employer has a retrospective premium arrangement with Insurer X, the employer may request that a specific stop-loss limit be included in the plan. This may not require an additional contract, but would be a part of the master contract that specifies the retrospective premium arrangement and the administrative aspects of the plan.

An employer may also purchase stop-loss insurance from another insurer. This might be necessary if the regular insurer does not offer an appropriate policy. Occasionally, an employer purchases a stop-loss policy from another insurer because the price is lower.

-334-

What is the difference between pooling and stop-loss insurance?

Both terms involve the same concept: protection for the employer against large losses in set time periods. Pooling is used to exclude large claims from an employer's claims experience so that when renewal rates are developed, fluctuations are not counted. Employers pay a pool charge to avoid this fluctuation and the resulting fluctuation in rates. Without pooling, the insurer would pay the claims and would also apply them toward the employer's loss ratio.

Stop-loss insurance is a term used in many different contexts, including as a synonym for out-of-pocket maximum by some insurers. However, technically it refers to a contractual agreement involved in most alternative funding arrangements. The protection requires the *insurer* to pay for claims in excess of predetermined limits. Without stop-loss insurance, the insurer would not be paying the excess claims, the employer would be.

-335-

Why does an employer's attitude toward risk affect the choice of plan funding?

An employer that is averse to risk is not a good candidate for alternative funding, which allows the employer to absorb some of the risk that the insurer assumes in conventionally funded plans. An employer that is unwilling or unable to absorb losses should probably retain conventional funding.

-336-

How do prior claims experience and the work-force health profile affect the choice of plan funding?

An employer with poor claims experience is unlikely to elect alternative funding because the employer assumes the liability for part or all of that risk. It is likely that experience that has been bad will continue to be bad, and if a group contains a lot of smokers, overweight employees, and individuals with high blood pressure, the likelihood of high medical claims is also high until those employees at risk leave the work force in significant numbers.

-337-

How is a deferred premium arrangement different from a conventionally funded plan?

This is the simplest of all alternative funding arrangements. Conventionally funded plans allow the employer a 31-day grace period during which premium for the current month is overdue but payable without allowing the policy to lapse. Insurers will defer premium receipt for certain employers by an additional 30 or 60 days, thus extending the grace period to 60 or 90 days. This enables the employer to retain funds for an extended period, thus allowing investment income on those funds to accrue to the employer rather than to the insurer. It also permits the policy to remain intact without payment of premium.

Since 90 days worth of premium is typically equivalent to the reserves required by the insurer, this deferred premium arrangement effectively eliminates the cash reserve usually held by the insurer. If the policy terminates, then all of the deferred premium is typically due as of the date of termination.

-338-

Why would an employer elect a deferred premium arrangement?

The employer's cash flow is improved because the employer is able to use the premium deferred in either that business or elsewhere.

-339-

Why don't all employers elect deferred premium arrangements?

Insurers do not provide deferred premium arrangements for most employers. This practice is essentially an extension of credit, and insurers are not inclined to underwrite that risk without protection, such as a letter of credit. In addition, the insurer charges a fee for its loss of income when premiums are deferred. The combination of the costs of determining and ensuring the credit worthiness of an employer plus the loss of investment income to the insurer results in an increased expense for the insurer and may produce a very small net saving for the employer.

-340-

How is a high self-insured deductible (HSID) plan different from a conventionally funded plan?

HSID plans allow the employer to self-fund the first tier of any individual's covered expenses for health care. The employer chooses an HSID level, such as $1,000, and pays covered expenses over the individual deductible for any insured who incurs claims, up to that $1,000 maximum. The plan design details are given by the insurance company, which typically provides eligibility review, claims processing, and the assumption of the risk above $1,000 per individual.

Most often, the insurance company processes claims for the high self-insured portion of the contract and advises the employer (in writing) what claims in what amounts the employer should pay.

-341-

Why would an employer elect an HSID plan?

Since HSID plans require less premium to the insurer for both current and future claims, the employer retains funds that would usually be paid to the insurance company, thereby improving its cash flow position. The employer must fund current claims up to the HSID level, but may be able to pay funds out less quickly than if the plan had been totally insured, depending on the timing of the claims. Also, if claims are less than would normally be expected, the employer will come out ahead. This is because the insurance company would have set premiums at a level to fund "expected claims"; thus, if the employer that elects an HSID plan beats the odds and experiences lower than expected claims, the employer will spend less.

The employer also would not be paying the insurer a premium to fund future claims liabilities on those individuals who incur claims less than or equal to the self-insured deductible amount in a plan year. The employer assumes that liability. The employer may also save money because it will pay the insurer no premium tax on the self-insured part of the plan. Therefore, even if the employer self-funds claims that are nearly equal to what the insurer would have expected, and thus pays out approximately the same money as would have been paid in premiums for the first tier of protection, the employer will save the premium tax.

Some employers save money by implementing HSID plans because their employees become more prudent purchasers of medical care. These companies make it clear to employees that when they are reimbursed for health care expenses under a certain level, they are being paid with employer money, not insurer money.

-342-

Why would an employer reject the HSID plan as an alternative funding arrangement?

An employer with an HSID plan could pay out more than for a conventionally funded plan in some years. Also, the additional administration, including employee benefits expertise, required by the employer may not be a cost the employer is willing to absorb. The employer could pay more, in total, for the HSID plan than for a conventionally insured plan when:

- Claims for which the employer is liable exceed expected levels, in which case fully insured premiums would have been a better investment, based on the fact that the insurer that accepts a fixed premium is not entitled to additional premium to fund higher than expected claims;
- Run-out claims liabilities for claims up to the HSID limit are excessive; or
- The employer uses a third-party administrator to administer claims and perform other services the insurer usually performs, and the combination of the TPA expenses plus the insurer's expenses is higher than the expenses would have been under a conventionally insured plan. This sometimes happens due to the split of services and extra coordination work done by the TPA and employer that traditionally is done by the insurer.

-343-

What kinds of employers elect HSID plans?

Employers that have more than 50 covered employees and are willing to absorb a piece of the risk usually taken by the insurer are the logical candidates. The employer must be able to absorb peaks of outgoing cash flow over months and years, and have administrative capability (electronic data processing) to track and accurately pay claims even though the actual claims review is almost always done by the insurer or a TPA.

Employers with more than 500 covered employees typically elect other funding alternatives that have the potential for greater savings.

-344-

How do retrospective premium arrangements differ from conventionally funded plans?

Under a "retro" agreement, the insurer agrees to collect less than the conventional premium from the employer. At the end of the year, the insurer has the right to collect additional premium from the employer if the actual loss ratio exceeds the loss ratio agreed to at the beginning of the retro agreement period. Typically, the initial premium reduction is equal to the margin built into the rate. The maximum additional premium payable is capped. It is agreed to at the beginning of the policy year, and may bring the total premium to more than would have been paid in the absence of the retro agreement.

In effect, the insurer is agreeing to collect premiums at the expected claims level, collecting no premium for fluctuation. If claims exceed the expected level, some or all of the retro may be "called."

-345-

Why would an employer negotiate a retrospective premium arrangement?

The employer retains funds it ordinarily would remit to the insurer during the year, thus improving its cash flow position. The employer assumes some additional risk if the retro agreement states that more than the conventional premium can be collected if claims exceed a set level, but this risk is limited because a maximum retro is agreed on at the beginning of the policy year.

-346-

Why might an employer not negotiate a retrospective premium arrangement?

An employer that implements a retro arrangement may find that the savings are minimal, due to the insurance company's increased retention charges. These charges include a charge for the loss of income the insurer will experience by collecting less premium during the policy year and a charge for assuming the credit risk of the employer. The employer may be required to pay additional premium at policy year end. If the retro agreement specifies that the collectible additional premium is capped, but at a level that makes the total potential premium higher than the conventional premium would have been, the employer can pay more than under a conventional plan.

-347-

To whom are retrospective premium arrangements available?

Insurers are unwilling to provide retrospective premium plans to employers with fewer than 50 covered employees and, in fact, rarely allow retro plans for employers with fewer than 150 employees. Retrospective premium arrangements are most often arranged for employers with between 200 and 500 employees whose past experience requires rates that the employer and intermediary believe are too high. They may negotiate a lower premium rate with the insurer by agreeing to pay a retro, but only if claims *do* accumulate to the insurer's original projections. To ensure that the retro will be paid if it is called, insurers will confirm the credit worthiness of the employer requesting a retrospective arrangement.

Some insurers are offering retrospective premium arrangements to small employers whose experience is habitually better than the manual pool. These employers, whose rates are based partially on experience and partially on manual rates, are becoming more willing to assume some of the risk the insurer has traditionally assumed. Rate increases may be necessary in general, due to increasing claims costs, but for small employers whose claims experience is better than average, a modified retro agreement may be available.

-348-

What is a reserve reduction agreement?

Agreements of this nature take two forms: (1) an upfront amendment to the insurance policy, which eliminates the insurer's liability after contract termination and (2) an agreement between employer and insurer that the employer will retain the reserves traditionally paid to the insurer, but the insurer will be liable for benefits after termination and the employer must return the reserves to the insurer. Both arrangements result in decreased premiums payable to the insurer.

-349-

Why would reserves decrease if an insurer eliminates its liability after contract termination?

Traditionally, the insurer is liable after contract termination for extended benefits for disabled employees and for claims incurred but unreported prior to termination. Some employers are willing to assume this liability, thereby eliminating the reserves held by the insurer. Furthermore, in states that have not enacted discontinuance and replacement regulations, employers are allowed to reduce or eliminate these benefits entirely. The insurer's requirements are thus reduced.

-350-

Why would an employer want to negotiate a reserve reduction?

Premiums decrease for employers that modify benefits payable upon contract termination or hold the reserves traditionally held by the insurer. This is especially true in the first year, when the insurer typically establishes reserves with a percentage of the initial premium.

-351-

Why might an employer not change the conventional reserve arrangement?

Some states prohibit the reduction or elimination of extended benefits. Even in those states that do not, most employers do not make this change, since a reduction of these benefits could negatively affect insureds.

When an employer holds the reserves usually paid to the insurer, the insurance company still typically retains liability for certain claims payments after contract termination. Therefore, the insurer must have access to the funds, and the employer may be required to provide them at a most inconvenient time. The insurer also typically requires some form of arrangement to protect its credit risk, such as a letter of credit from a bank, for which there is a charge. This may be in addition to the maintenance of the minimum balance in an account where the reserves or a portion of the reserves will be held.

Some arrangements *require* the employer to invest the funds (the amount of the conventional reserve requirement) in certain accessible securities; the employer may not be allowed to use the captured reserves as working capital in the business, because of the risk of loss and the inaccessibility of funds. This arrangement is agreed to by employer and insurer, and although the funds are the employer's property, the insurer has the contractual right to withdraw money to fund obligations after contract termination.

The administration required for these arrangements can be cumbersome. Furthermore, an insurer may be unwilling to allow the employer to retain reserves, based on an assessment of the employer's credit worthiness and the practical effectiveness of letters of credit.

-352-

What employers typically implement reserve reduction agreements?

The release of reserves to an employer is rarely available to smaller employers. The additional administration involved requires that a significant reserve amount be involved, in order for the employer to net savings. And generally, the smaller the employer, the less the benefits expertise. Administration of the banking arrangements requires a knowledgeable employer and intermediary. Also, few employers, especially smaller, relatively paternal employers, modify extended benefits provisions; as a result, the advantages of releasing reserves due to discontinuing benefits are rarely realized.

-353-

How does a minimum premium plan (MPP) differ from conventional funding?

MPPs are partially self-funded plans. The employer assumes responsibility for funding most benefits, and the insurer assumes liability for benefits above a predetermined level. Premiums are reduced significantly, because the insurer is responsible for funding only a small portion of benefits. Two kinds of MPPs are most common:

(1) The insurer is liable for benefits obligations after termination of the MPP contract and thus holds reserves similar to those required under a conventionally insured plan; or

(2) The employer is liable for benefits obligations after termination of the MPP contract and, thus, the insurer does not hold reserves to fund this liability.

-354-

At what level does the insurer become responsible for benefits funding under an MPP?

The employer and insurer establish a "trigger point" beyond which the insurer is liable. This liability can be set on a monthly cumulative basis or on an annual basis. The trigger is negotiated between each employer and insurer, based on expected claims. A trigger point of 125% of expected claims is one example.

Under a monthly cumulative arrangement, the employer is protected against fluctuation in claims from month to month. If cumulative claims exceed the monthly trigger point, the insurer pays claims from its own funds. In a subsequent month, if claims are below the trigger, the insurer is usually allowed to recoup the amount from the employer to cover the payments made in the month when claims exceeded the trigger point. For example:

Month	*Employer Obligation*	*Claims*	*Employer Pays*	*Insurer Pays*	*Unexpended Employer Funds*
1	$ 100	$ 60	$ 60	$ 0	$40
2	200	70	70	0	70
3	300	120	120	0	50
4	400	150	150	0	0
5	500	100	100	0	0
6	600	110	100	10	0
7	700	40	40	−10	50
8	800	100	100	0	50
9	900	130	130	0	20
10	1,000	50	50	0	70
11	1,100	180	170	10	0
12	1,200	140	100	40	0

Under an annual arrangement, the employer funds all claims until the annual trigger point is reached. For example:

Month	*Employer Obligation*	*Claims*	*Employer Pays*	*Insurer Pays*	*Unexpended Employer Funds*
1	$1,200	$ 60	$ 60	$ 0	$1,140
2	1,200	70	70	0	1,070
3	1,200	120	120	0	950
4	1,200	150	150	0	800
5	1,200	100	100	0	700
6	1,200	110	110	0	590
7	1,200	40	40	0	550
8	1,200	100	100	0	450
9	1,200	130	130	0	320
10	1,200	50	50	0	270
11	1,200	180	180	0	90
12	1,200	140	90	50	0

The insurer's and employer's obligations for funding under both arrangements are the same, in amounts, by the end of the year. Just the timing is different.

-355-

If an individual incurs a shock claim under an MPP, does the full amount of that claim count toward the employer's trigger point?

Whether the full amount will count toward the trigger point depends on whether an arrangement has been made to "stop the employer's losses" at a certain point per insured per policy year. Some employers elect to pay the insurer a fee for this protection. For example, if the insurer agreed to assume the full risk for the portion of any individual claims in a year that exceeded $50,000, the employer would pay a monthly fee for this protection.

-356-

How are claims paid with employer funds under an MPP?

The employer establishes a bank account to which the insurer has access to pay claims. The account is funded as claims are submitted for payment, except that one to three days of expected claims are required to be maintained in the account. Claims analysis is typically performed by the insurer, although some employers use third-party administrators instead, who would have access to the funds, just as the insurer would if it were the administrator.

-357-

Why would an employer benefit from establishing an MPP?

The employer retains significant funds under an MPP, paying the insurer only for administrative expenses, reserves (unless the employer holds the reserves), and predetermined premium for claims above the trigger point. In the first year, when the insurer establishes reserves, premium could be as much as 35% of the conventionally insured premium, but in later years, premium could be as little as 7% of the conventionally insured level, covering only administration, change in reserves due to change in claims levels, and excess claims premium.

Premium tax is usually not payable for the noninsured portion of the risk, but some states do hold that an insurance company's obligations to pay premium tax are not changed for MPPs. In this case, the employer pays premium tax to the insurer, which, in turn, remits it to the state insurance department. Usually, an agreement for this contingency is reached initially. Most insurers require a "hold-harmless" agreement that relieves the insurer of any obligations for taxes a state might assess in the future that the employer had not previously paid. (Hold-harmless agreements are also used when insurers need assurance that an employer will release reserves it has been holding in various funding arrangements.)

Employers can save money on MPPs if claims are lower than expected, because the premium they would have paid an insurer would have exceeded funds necessary to cover claims. However, while employers may save money in one year because claims are lower than expected, claims in subsequent years usually balance out the "good" years in the long run. Thus, the savings are usually realized not from positive claims experience but from decreased premium taxes and from investment income.

-358-

Why wouldn't an employer elect an MPP?

Employers that elect MPP arrangements assume most of the risk traditionally assumed by the insurer. This can result in increased cost of the health care plan, if claims regularly exceed expected amounts. In addition, the administrative work required to establish and maintain the banking arrangements requires expertise and effort too burdensome for some employers.

The insurer's risk charges may be substantial for some employers whose credit worthiness is questionable, especially if a letter of credit is used, which is expensive to arrange. The employer may not realize a net savings by establishing an MPP.

-359-

What employers typically elect an MPP?

Employers with MPPs usually have at least $250,000 in annual premium. Employers whose plans involve less premium than this are usually not underwritten for MPPs by insurers. Insurers also require some protection against the credit risk an MPP represents. Thus, if an employer cannot supply a letter of credit or an equivalent instrument at a reasonable cost, an MPP may not be an alternative.

-360-

How are third-party administrative services used in an MPP?

An employer may elect to have administration, including claims determination, performed by a source other than the insurer, if the service the TPA can provide is better or less expensive. In this situation, the insurer only assumes risk, and the TPA provides documentation to the insurer for claims payments for which the insurer is liable over the trigger point.

-361-

Do some employers elect to insure the entire risk of a health care plan?

Some very large employers may elect to fully self-fund. Depending on their risk capacity, even these employers may purchase some form of stop-loss insurance. When an employer elects to fully self-fund a plan but have an insurer administer it, a contract for administrative services only (ASO) may be arranged. Some employers prefer to administer everything but the claims. This arrangement is known as claims services only (CSO).

Group Health Insurance Plan Administration

Proper administration of the health insurance plan is essential if the employer and employee are to receive maximum value. Plan administration begins before the effective date of the plan and continues throughout the plan year and during the renewal period. This chapter examines plan administration and covers such topics as employee enrollment, claims filing, billing procedures, and the renewal process.

-362-

After an employer selects a health insurance plan, what must be done to put the coverage into effect?

After receiving the plan quotes and selecting the plan, the employer makes an official written application and pays a binder that approximates the first month's premium to the selected insurer. (This is commonly referred to as the "app and check.") A worksheet usually accompanies the application. It provides a precise explanation of all the information that is required for smooth operation of the plan. This includes, but is not limited to, the legal name of the policyholder and the locations of employees who will be insured, classes of employees eligible for coverage, the effective date of the plan, details of the coverage requested, the parameters for employee contributions and policyholder premium payment, the claims payment method, and the intermediary involved.

In addition to the app and check, enrollment of employees must take place before the underwriter will approve coverage (except the group as a risk) and issue a final premium rate. This is because changes in enrollment can significantly affect the cost of the plan. Thus, the employees are told about the new coverage and required to enroll prior to final approval by the insurer.

-363-

Is the coverage effective as soon as the insurer receives the application and enrollment material?

No. The enrollment forms accompany the application materials to the insurance company's home office, where the underwriter reviews the enrollment and the final coverage requested. This pre-issue work typically occurs during the month prior to the effective date of the coverage, although the extra preparation required for implementation of some plans, such as flexible benefits, must be done several months earlier. Only after the final review and approval by the insurer is the coverage effective.

-364-

When might an underwriter not approve a policy for coverage?

There are two general reasons that an underwriter would not approve the policy. When the coverage details are substantially different from the plan the underwriter had originally agreed to, thus materially changing the risk, the plan may not be approved as submitted. The second reason for nonapproval would be if the group's enrollment produces a substantially different final group than expected. For example, because 75% of all *eligible* employees are usually required to participate in the plan, a plan that has apparently enrolled only 60% of eligible employees would not be approved. The employer in this situation had provided the insurer with a census listing of *all* employees rather than only those eligible. As a result, the underwriter developed a plan and rates actually based on 80%-90% of all employees enrolling.

-365-

If a policy is not approved by the home-office underwriter, what happens?

Usually, the intermediary and group representative work together to make changes to the plan or the premium that make the group an acceptable risk for the underwriter. Obviously, it is in the insurer's best interests to make the plan workable. Nonetheless, insurers do have specific underwriting criteria that they must follow in order to remain solvent.

-366-

Why does the insurance company require detailed coverage information before issuing the policy?

It is important that the master contract reflect precisely the coverage desired, because claims are paid on the basis of the contract. Also, the final premium rate is developed from the enrollment and application material; so the information must be accurate. Although the underwriter may have quite a detailed record of what coverage is desired and who is likely to participate, based on the materials submitted for an initial quote, the final master contract must be developed from current information.

Another reason for the detailed coverage information is that some insurers allow policies with fewer than 100 employees to be "field underwritten." This means that the initial quote is developed by a field sales representative. As a result, the home office may have had no prior knowledge of the employee group, and the application and enrollment forms may be the first things the underwriter sees about the group.

-367-

Who provides the announcement materials necessary to inform the employees about the plan?

Typically, a concise letter from the employer to employees explains what benefits the new plan will provide, who is eligible to enroll, how much an employee's monthly contribution will be (if the plan is contributory), and when the coverage will become effective. An insurance company representative may provide form letters to the policyholder that can be customized to meet the employer's needs. Both employer and insurer generally hope that as many employees enroll as possible, and thus the announcement materials are often a joint effort.

-368-

Why is enrollment in the plan encouraged?

The employer is attempting to meet the employees' coverage needs by providing a health care plan. If employees aren't educated about the plan and encouraged to enroll, the employer will not be providing the desired benefits. Further, because a larger insured group sometimes results in a better spread of risk, the rates may be better as enrollment increases. Administrative charges by the insurer also may reflect economies of scale in the rates.

The insurer wants to enroll as many employees as possible because its spread of risk improves as the insured pool increases in size.

-369-

What information must individuals provide to enroll in the plan?

The insurer provides the employer with enrollment forms to obtain some or all of the following information from enrollees:

- Name;
- Sex;
- Age;
- Social Security number;
- Salary;
- Occupation (rarely required for health care coverage);
- Election or rejection of coverage (if contributory);
- Marital status and election or rejection of dependent coverage (if contributory);
- Dependents to be covered (many policies do not require this);
- Selection of coverage if there is more than one offered;
- The employee's beneficiary for the life insurance that usually accompanies health coverage; and
- Authorization for payroll deductions (for contributory plans).

This information is more detailed and accurate than the census data provided to the insurer for the initial quote.

-370-

Must individuals enroll in a noncontributory plan?

Yes. Although the employer knows that everyone will be covered, demographic information and beneficiary designation (for life insurance coverage) is necessary for the insurer to develop a final premium rate and, for some plans, to establish the employee records needed to pay claims.

-371-

Who enrolls the employees in the group health insurance plan?

The company's employee benefits administrator may request the intermediary or insurance representative to help with the enrollment, but small employers may not need help because of the limited number of employees. A meeting is sometimes planned for all eligible employees in which the plan is explained and the enrollment forms are distributed.

-372-

How long do employees have to complete their enrollment cards?

Because the enrollment forms must be submitted to the insurance company before the effective date of the plan, employees are encouraged to return them as quickly as possible. An arbitrary time period for form return, such as a week, is typically established by the employer. Employees who submit forms late may or may not be allowed to participate in the plan as of the effective date of the plan.

-373-

Why would an employee who submits a late enrollment form not be allowed to participate as of the plan's effective date?

Insurance companies have established rules regarding late enrollment in order to ensure consistent, accurate premium and coverage records, and to protect the plan against adverse selection. Whether the employee obtains coverage as of the plan effective date depends on how late the form is submitted. If the insurer does not have the form before the effective date, the employee is typically added to the plan on the date the form is received, if that is within 31 days of the effective date. If the employee does not enroll within 31 days of becoming eligible, it is assumed that he or she has declined coverage. Insurers try to have employees return enrollment forms that note if they are actually declining coverage in order to keep accurate records, and to ensure that no employee is inadvertently excluded from enrollment in the plan.

-374-

If an employee declines coverage initially, can he or she enroll at a later date?

For contributory plans, an employee who initially declines coverage, whether as of the initial effective date of the plan or as of his or her initial eligibility date (a new hire or an employee who becomes part of an eligible class after the initial plan effective date), must supply evidence of insurability in order to enroll in the plan later. This is because an employee may elect health care coverage only after he or she has been injured or has become ill. This antiselection can significantly increase the medical claims on a plan and, if allowed to occur repeatedly, can threaten insurer solvency.

Even if an individual presents evidence of insurability that is acceptable to the insurer, most plans limit coverage for conditions that existed before the individual's enrollment date.

-375-

Can employees submit claims after the effective date of the plan but before they receive their certificates of insurance?

Yes. Claims for medical care received after the plan effective date (other than those resulting from a preexisting condition not covered by the plan) can be submitted and paid as soon as the underwriter approves the policy and the enrollment information is filed at the home office of the insurer. The period between the effective date and delivery of the contract and certificates of insurance is kept as short as possible.

-376-

What is a certificate of insurance?

Once the plan becomes effective, a certificate of insurance is given to each employee. The certificate resembles the master contract and summarizes the plan coverage. Although certificates are not required in all states, certificates provide employees with a summary of the coverage parameters, just as the master contract does for the employer. (The "cert" does not constitute a contract between the cert holder and the insurer.)

Some insurers also provide covered employees with booklets that describe coverage in less technical language than the master contract. These booklets are not filed with the state insurance department as certificates are often required to be. Booklets explain coverage in readable language and are becoming increasingly common, due in part to state "readability" laws. It is also common for insurers to provide "cert booklets" that have both a technical coverage explanation and a layperson's explanation under one cover.

-377-

What other materials are issued to employees?

Many plans include identification cards so that each employee has a simple wallet-sized card to refer to when questioned by a provider or when filing a claim. Many employers purchase hospital guarantee cards from their insurers as part of their plans instead of ID cards. The guarantee card typically ensures that a hospital will accept a patient even if the hospital cannot reach the insurance company to verify coverage. Cards usually guarantee coverage for 72 hours, and are meant to serve as temporary coverage confirmation on weekends and holidays when a provider would not be able to contact the insurer. Cards are usually provided to covered dependents as well as employees.

If the health care plan includes a prescription drug card plan, employees are issued cards as soon as possible after the effective date of the policy. The prescription drug administrator produces those cards and often ships them directly to the employer. The employer can specify that it wants cards only for employees or cards for both covered dependents and employees. Some employers publish a guide to participating pharmacies that will accept the card.

Various other materials are distributed, especially when a new policy provision is being added. If new limitations are being placed on coverage or if expansions are being made to coverage, employers and insurers want to communicate the changes so that employees understand what benefits will be payable. For example, if utilization review (UR) is added to the health plan, employees will need to understand when they must contact the UR agent, where to call or write, and what the ramifications will be if they don't follow the UR procedures.

Another example of additional materials involves preferred provider organizations. In order for an employee to visit a preferred provider, he or she must know who those providers are. The insurance company or third-party administrator publishes a list of the preferred provders periodically, because additions and deletions are made during the year.

-378-

What administrative material does the insurer initially provide to the employer?

The employer is usually given a supply of enrollment forms, certificates, and booklets for additional enrollees; premium reporting forms; claims forms; the master contract; a final covered employee listing; and an administrative manual.

-379-

How are employers billed for group health insurance premiums?

There are two kinds of billing arrangements between employers and insurers for group health insurance premiums: self-accounting and home-office billing.

Self-accounting billing allows the employer to calculate premium due based on changes that have occurred since the last premium due date, such as employee additions and terminations. The insurer receives only a summary of the changes, rather than an itemized listing. Some insurers generate reminder bills for self-accounting employers, but these typically provide only a recap of the prior period's changes and premium.

Most large employers are required to use self-accounting because of the significant number of changes that are likely to occur from month to month. The insurer prefers not to keep track of employee additions, terminations, and status changes (e.g., addition of dependents), because many of the employees of a large company will never file a claim, and thus the insurer has no need to keep information of those insureds in its system. Further, most large companies have sophisticated payroll systems that can produce monthly reports with changes automatically translated to changes in premium, making it unnecessary for the insurer to do this work.

Smaller employers that elect home-office accounting are required to submit individual changes in insured status to the insurer so that accurate bills can be generated from the insurance company's home office. For example, when a new employee is hired and completes an enrollment form, the form is submitted to the insurer, and the insurer establishes a file on that employee, thereby increasing the required monthly premium. A bill reflecting that will be produced for the coming period. The initial enrollment forms provide the insurer with the information required for computerized claims payment and billing.

As employers' electronic data processing systems become more sophisticated, less billing will be done on paper. Compatible systems can allow the insurer access to the enrollment changes electronically, and premium can even be transferred over the phone from the employer's bank account to the insurer's.

-380-

Whom can an employer contact for help in calculating premium payments?

A service representative of the insurance company located in one of the insurer's field offices can be contacted by phone. Some insurers provide their policyholders with the name of their billing representative in the home office.

-381-

If an employer's premium payment is late, does coverage lapse?

Generally, policyholders have 31 days from the premium due date to remit the premium. However, if the insurer does not receive the premium by that date, the coverage usually is not canceled immediately. Instead, the insurer attempts to collect the premium by sending late notices and then a formal cancellation notice assuming, until proven otherwise, that the employer does wish to maintain coverage. Insurance companies have different time requirements and procedures regarding late premium payment.

Usually the employer does pay the late premium, thus reinstating the policy, and claims are paid. If the employer does not remit premiums, and the insurer has made it clear when those premiums must be paid to avoid policy termination, the policy is terminated.

-382-

Does the insurer periodically audit employers that self-account?

Yes. Audits are done randomly or for employers that have requested help to solve a significant billing problem. The audits are performed in order to ensure that the employer is comfortable with the administrative requirements for the policy, especially enrollment of employees and premium payment.

Proper enrollment of employees is crucial to claims payment. The administrator must understand when employees can be enrolled with and without evidence of insurability, when coverage becomes effective, and when premium payments must start in order to ensure coverage. Audits help the insurer understand what needs to be more clearly explained to administrators to facilitate smooth plan operation, in addition to helping individual employers that may be having problems with their administration.

-383-

How does an individual submit a claim for payment?

The information regarding the medical expense must be provided to the insurer or the third-party administrator for review. This can be communicated on a claims form or electronically, depending on the provider's and insurer's or administrator's procedures. The majority of private insurers require that the insured obtain a claims form from the employer, have the provider complete information about the care provided, and then submit it to the insurer for payment. This is known as a "direct claim" because the employer does not become involved in certifying eligibility; the claim goes directly from employee to insurer. Of course, for direct claim policies, the insurer must be continually updated about enrollment changes.

Some employers require that an insured request a form from the benefits administrator, who certifies eligibility by signing the form before it is provided to the employee. The insurer should not have to ascertain eligibility for these insureds, since the employer has already done so.

Some plans require no claims forms for employees. For example, an employee may present a card to the health care provider. The provider submits charges directly to the insurer for services rendered to the insured. Usually, the card shows what coverage the employee has, and the provider knows what is billable. Sometimes services for which there is only partial coverage are provided. In that case, the insured is billed for the balance when the provider has been paid only a partial amount by the insurer.

A relatively new approach to claims submission is for the employer or insurer to provide the employee with a medical credit card that the employee presents to the provider at the time care is provided. In essence, this approach is like the prescription drug card process, but the complexity of health care coverage requires a great deal more administration and presents special risks to both the insurer and the employer. This approach has not gained widespread acceptance to date, but because the paper work for the employee is all but eliminated, this kind of arrangement is growing in popularity.

-384-

Do most individuals pay the health care provider for the service and receive reimbursement later from the insurer?

Providers either receive payment from the insured at the time of service or accept a claims form or card as evidence of coverage. In the latter situation, the employee is asked to "assign benefits" to the provider, thus avoiding payment at the time of service. This practice originated from medical care providers' need for assurance of payment for services rendered. Some insureds requested reimbursement from their insurer but didn't pay the provider with the money they received, thus creating cash flow and bad debt problems for the providers.

Recently, more providers have required payment by the insured at the time of service, rather than simply being assured of receipt of reimbursement from the insurer later. This eliminates bookkeeping for the provider because the claims forms are submitted by the insured, although the insured usually must get an explanation of the service rendered and a signature from the provider in order for the claim to be paid by the insurer. It also improves the provider's cash flow.

In an emergency situation, an insured with a guarantee card from the insurer is in a better position to receive care without administrative annoyances.

-385-

What is assignment of benefits?

The insured authorizes the insurance company to pay any benefits directly to the provider of medical care, rather than to the insured.

-386-

Whom can an employee ask for help in completing a claims form?

The employer's benefits administrator can usually help employees, but many insurers can also provide assistance. A toll-free number is sometimes provided by the insurer for benefits questions.

-387-

Can employees determine whether a claim will be paid before they receive the medical care?

This is a prudent practice, and one that is becoming more widespread due to changes in benefits programs that find some expenses not covered. The employee benefits administrator should help employees understand how the deductible and coinsurance work and interpret the insurance booklet. The intermediary or insurer can be called if there is some question about an expense.

This pre-claims review is an excellent idea, but employees are always cautioned by the insurer that the actual claim determines what will finally be paid. General statements regarding coverage can be made, but until the actual claim is submitted, eligibility is ascertained, and the claim circumstances are reviewed, the insurer cannot be absolutely sure that certain expenses will be covered.

-388-

How quickly are insureds reimbursed for their claims expenses?

Claims turnaround time varies by insurer from several days to several months. The information an insurer requires in order to determine reimbursement is sometimes detailed and comes from various sources. Errors and omissions may cause delay. Providers are sometimes asked to provide additional information when the claims form is completed improperly, or the reasons for the procedures and charges are unclear. If benefits are to be coordinated with other insurance programs, information from other insurers must be requested in order to determine each insurer's payment.

-389-

Who receives the benefits check?

If the employee has assigned benefits to a provider, the provider is paid directly; otherwise, the employee receives the payment. Often, checks are mailed directly to the insured. Some employers prefer to receive the checks from the insurer, and distribute them to employees. If reimbursement is for a service received by a dependent, the insured (the employee) receives the payment. An explanation of benefits (EOB) accompanies the check.

-390-

What is an EOB?

An EOB summarizes how a reimbursement was determined. It usually includes the services provided, the providers involved, the date of the care, and an explanation of what services were covered or not covered. If payment is made directly to a provider, a facsimile of the check is often provided to the insured, with an EOB. Typically, the EOB material also explains how the claims appeal process works. ERISA requires this explanation whenever a claim is denied.

-391-

Why would an employee appeal a claims determination?

An employee may disagree with all or part of the insurer's payment calculation or the denial of certain charges as covered expenses.

-392-

How does an employee appeal a claims determination?

ERISA regulations establish and define the appeal process for both insurer and employee. Generally, by law, the claimant can be required to complete reasonable forms for the insurer. Claimants have at least 60 days to appeal claims, and the insurer or plan administrator must answer the appeal within 60 days. If a claim is denied, the insured must be provided with a written explanation of the reasons for the denial and references to the policy provision on which the denial is based. This procedure is followed for initial claims denial as well as for an appeal denial.

-393-

How does an employer renew its health insurance policy?

The insurer assumes that the policyholder wants to renew its policy and maintain the same plan design unless it hears differently from the employer's intermediary. Thus, policy renewal can be as simple as the insurer rerating the group to determine a premium rate for the coming policy period (typically a year) and sending the notice of the renewal rates to the policyholder or intermediary.

Small employers whose policies are manually rated have little premium negotiation to deal with. Unless they request a plan change, such as an increase in deductible or the addition of utilization review service, the coverage will remain in force as it has been, although the rate may change. If the insurer does not have an up-to-date employee census listing, the employer will be asked to submit one three months before the policy anniversary date, so that a new policy rate may be calculated. A notice must be sent to the policyholder before the policy anniversary date, based on the contractual agreement regarding the timing required for premium changes.

For employers with more than 50 covered employees, the renewal process usually involves an analysis of the policy period's claims in order to develop the experience-rated portion of the rate. For more complicated policies, such as collectively bargained groups and flexible benefits, the renewal process involves more negotiation on benefits and rates, and the process must start earlier, even if the first phase is only collection of information on the insureds and the claims history.

-394-

When can an employer change its coverage?

Plan changes can be made at any time, given the insurer's approval. The employer discusses needs with the intermediary, and a request is made to the insurer for the change in premium that would result from a change in coverage.

The insurer can make plan changes for the employer at any time, but the most common point is coincident with renewal. Typically, the underwriter develops a renewal rate based on the in-force plan, and then calculates a different rate based on the proposed changes. Often, the request for a plan change follows an underwriter's premium rate change notice. In recent years, the rates for most policies have increased, even when claims experience was good, because of the trend component. Thus, employers have been looking for plan changes that will decrease their rates.

-395-

What kinds of changes do employers make at renewal?

Recently, the most common changes have been changes from a base plus plan to a comprehensive plan, increases in deductibles and coinsurance, and the implementation of other cost-management provisions (see the chapter entitled "Managing Health Insurance Costs"). The decision to implement these provisions usually results from the underwriter's review and communication to the intermediary or policyholder of the claims utilization patterns.

-396-

When the policy is renewed, are all employees automatically covered?

Only employees who have previously enrolled are automatically covered. Others, known as "late enrollees," would have to submit evidence of insurability.

-397-

If an employer believes that a renewal rate is too high, what options are available?

The intermediary can attempt to negotiate a decrease to the renewal rate or get quotes from other carriers.

-398-

What kinds of plan changes might an employer want to make during the plan year?

An employer might want to implement cost-management provisions in the middle of a plan year due to concern that the renewal rate will call for a large increase. Employers that are going through significant organizational changes or experiencing economic difficulties may choose to make changes immediately, rather than waiting for renewal.

-399-

Can an employer terminate coverage in the middle of a plan year?

Yes, but the employer will be held responsible for all premiums due and unpaid up to the official termination date. The request for termination must be in writing and dated prior to the requested termination date.

-400-

If an employer terminates coverage, what protection do employees have against medical expenses?

Normally, there is no gap in coverage for employees. If an employer terminates coverage, another insurer has usually been lined up to pick up the protection as of the minute the other insurer is terminated.

-401-

If an employee is not actively at work on the date the new coverage takes effect, will he or she be covered?

Employees who are on vacation or who are on a leave of absence are usually covered administratively, but this provision varies by insurer. Protection for employees who are not at work because they are disabled varies by state and by insurer. Some states require that the new insurer guarantee coverage for employees who were insured under a prior plan. Some insurers provide continuation of coverage for disabled employees even if the employer's state (situs of the policy) does not require this. "Continuity of coverage" and "preexisting conditions limitations'' provisions should be carefully reviewed before changing insurance carriers.

-402-

If an employee terminates employment, what protection does he or she have against medical expenses?

Some states require continuation of coverage for a certain period of employees who are terminated by the employer. In most cases, however, those who terminate employment, either involuntarily or voluntarily, become insured under the new employer's plan or elect a conversion policy from the previous employer's insurer.

-403-

What is a conversion privilege?

Individuals insured under a group plan (in most policies, they must have been insured for at least three months) can convert to an individual policy. Individuals eligible for similar group coverage under another plan are typically not allowed to convert. Coverage is available to the employee as well as to his or her dependents.

The individual often has several plans to choose from, but rarely do these options include a better plan than the group plan. Many states require that insurers offer a conversion privilege to help employees avoid gaps in coverage when they are between jobs.

-404-

Are there reports that the employer must file with the state or federal government regarding its health plan?

Employers with 100 or more covered employees must file a summary plan description (SPD) with the U.S. Department of Labor within 120 days after the plan is initiated. The plan administrator (usually the policyholder) is responsible for this action. If changes are made to the plan that affect the information in the SPD or materially affect the plan, a filing must be made within 210 days after the close of the plan year in which the modification was made.

-405-

What is a summary plan description?

An SPD furnishes the Department of Labor with specific information about the health plan. It includes the name and address of the policyholder; the type of benefits plan; the name, address, and telephone number of the plan administrator; the name and address of the person designated as agent for service of legal process; and the names and addresses of the plan trustees, if any. It also includes eligibility requirements, contribution requirements, claims processing procedures, benefits denial parameters, and an explanation of the appeals process. Each plan participant, as well as the Department of Labor, is provided with an SPD.

-406-

When an employer uses a TPA, what services does the administrator provide?

The administrator may take care of changes in enrollment, premium payment, and claims determination. When the TPA also acts as an intermediary, plan change and renewal administration would be included. Depending on how much of the plan is self-funded, the TPA will perform various parts of the work that the insurer does for a conventionally insured plan.

Future Trends in Health Insurance

Previous chapters addressed alternatives available to employers in such areas as design, cost management, funding, and administration of group health insurance plans. However, we are living in a very dynamic society, especially when it comes to health care and employee benefits. An employer that wants its employees to receive the greatest value for benefits dollars spent should be monitoring the developments in these fields and deciding when it makes sense to take advantage of them. This chapter discusses those trends that are likely to have an impact on employee benefits packages in the future.

-407-

What sources of group insurance may be available in the future, in addition to today's intermediaries?

Experiments are being conducted for distribution of insurance products in a variety of new ways. Many of these involve only individual insurance products, but group insurance may eventually follow. Some new distribution sources are banks, securities companies, department stores, direct mail, and hospital corporations. This may require greater expertise on the part of the buyer in order to make wise purchases, and could increase the cost of plans.

-408-

How is Blue Cross/Blue Shield changing?

BC/BS is changing in a number of ways. As described earlier, it is offering comprehensive plans in addition to the traditional base plus plans. Also, many nonprofit BC/BS organizations are setting up for-profit subsidiaries that include HMOs, TPAs, and other related businesses.

Traditionally, Blue Cross has covered hospital expenses, and Blue Shield has covered other expenses. Many BC/BS organizations in a given area are now merging into one entity, which is intended to decrease the administrative costs and difficulties that many employers and employees have encountered with the Blues.

The nonprofit tax status of BC/BS is being questioned. In addition, states have enacted legislation that limits the hospital discounts that can be negotiated by BC/BS to the savings realized by the way they do business (for example, having open enrollment periods during which all applicants are accepted regardless of health, and paying bills within a certain time period). The same discounts must be available to all third-party payers that perform similarly. The effect of such legislation will be that providers that discounted the price of their services to the Blues and then made up the difference by charging private insurance companies more will now charge everyone more equitably. Private insurers will be able to compete more effectively because the price discounts will not be as large. The Blues will also have to become more efficient because the price differential—previously a strong competitive advantage—will be less.

-409-

What will the work force look like 10 years from now?

The changes already taking place in the composition of the work force can be expected to continue. There will be even greater diversity in life styles and, therefore, needs. The average age of today's work force has gone down as a result of large numbers of workers of the baby-boom generation moving in. However, as that generation grows older, the average age of the American worker will again increase. Furthermore, since the generation after the baby boomers is much smaller, a shortage of labor is expected to develop. This will result in many retired people returning to the work force, especially as longevity increases and elderly people remain vigorous longer.

-410-

What effect is the continued diversity and aging of the work force expected to have on benefits?

As the work force changes and ages, employees will demand benefits that are of value to them. For example, as employees marry and have children, day-care benefits may become increasingly important. Older employees whose children are grown may seek increased medical benefits to pay for health care expenses, which are sure to rise as people age.

Employers must recognize that employees will also be seeking to make their own decisions, and that health plans that allow employees to choose will proliferate. Although such plans are obviously in the best interests of employees, they can be beneficial to employers as well, in terms of recruiting and retaining employees.

In addition, many new insurance products will be available through employers' benefits plans. Some are available today on a limited basis and will be expanded as employers demand them. They include coverage for such services as legal assistance; financial planning; retraining; and retiree health care, with special emphasis on coverage for long-term care.

-411-

What is a prepaid legal plan, and why is it important?

As the complexity of our society has increased, practical access to the legal system has decreased. Although it's believed that 80% of all legal problems can be handled quickly and inexpensively, most people don't take action because they're not sure they have a legal problem, don't know whom to call, or are afraid of the cost. A prepaid legal plan can handle anything from telephone legal service for simple problems to a full indemnity plan for a variety of legal services at a relatively low cost. Amounts contributed by an employer to a qualified group legal services plan were excludable from taxable income until the end of 1985, and that exclusion is expected to be extended to allow study of the effect of such plans on future taxable income.

-412-

Why might an employer offer financial planning in a group insurance plan?

The number of middle-income Americans who are investing part of their income in a variety of security instruments is increasing. They are seeking ways to make their dollars work more effectively for them in order to provide future security. Relatively few are knowledgeable about investments, and they need assistance with the dizzying number of new financial products available in today's marketplace. Many insurance companies offer the service, mostly to individuals.

-413-

What does retraining coverage mean?

As the pace of technological change accelerates, there is a growing need to retrain those members of the work force whose jobs are made obsolete. There is a corresponding need for employers and employees to plan for and allocate resources to this process, and effectively address the problems of the displaced worker.

-414-

Why has health care coverage for retirees become an issue?

The population as a whole continues to age. The number of people over age 65 is expected to grow from 29 million in 1985 to 35 million in 2000—almost 13% of the population. The number of people over age 85—2.7 million in 1985— is expected to reach 5 million in the year 2000. The cost of care for people in these age groups continues to increase, and the need for coverage for the low-income elderly is also increasing.

Almost half of current health insurance plans cancel coverage for employees upon retirement. For many of these people, Medicare is their only coverage, and it pays only about 50% of an individual's bill on average. Medicaid varies by state, but generally requires exhaustion of almost all private resources before coverage is funded. Many employers have felt the responsibility to fund health care coverage after retirement, but some new issues have been raised recently:

- The number of individuals requiring intermediate and custodial care or skilled nursing for longer periods has increased significantly, at a cost of $55 to $75 a day.
- New accounting disclosure rules have made management, especially in large companies, more aware of the cost of retiree benefits and its effect on bottom-line results.
- Prefunding of health insurance plans is permitted on a tax-deductible basis while employees are working, but investment income on the funds is taxable. This means that although contributions to the plan for coverage in future years are tax deductible, the income earned on that amount through investments while it is being accumulated is taxable. This situation makes prefunding benefits less attractive. However, if many people lose retiree benefits because of business failure, plan discontinuance, or early retirement, there may be legislation requiring prefunding.
- Court decisions have restricted the rights of employers to reduce or modify post-retirement benefits for already retired employees.

• There is some consideration being given to requiring employers to cover retirees under their health insurance plans. This would reduce the cost of the government's Medicare system, which is being stretched to its limit. The result of such legislation would be an increase in employers' health insurance costs, which most likely would be passed along to current employees.

-415-

What are the special issues connected with long-term care?

It is estimated that 65% of those people over age 85 and 25% of those over age 65 will need long-term care in their lifetimes. Because of the mobility of the population and varying life styles, family support systems have been reduced, and more institutional care will therefore be necessary. Generally, neither group insurance plans that continue after retirement nor Medicare provides coverage for long-term care, except in a facility that provides skilled medical care. Even then, coverage is usually for only a limited period of time. However, many individuals require intermediate or custodial care. Insurance companies have just begun to respond with individual policies that address the special needs of elderly former employees.

-416-

What other group insurance coverages may employees be asking for?

Group automobile and group homeowners' insurance are offered by several insurance companies today. The premium for these coverages is considered taxable income, but the advantages of paying for them on a payroll-deduction basis are expected to cause greater interest in the future.

-417-

How is the tax status of health insurance premiums being questioned?

In recent years, some legislators have proposed taxing employer contributions to group health insurance plans. Presently, such contributions are deductible as an ordinary and necessary business expense for employers and are not included as taxable income to employees. However, because of the large federal budget deficits, including employer contributions for health insurance as taxable income to employees is being investigated as a way to increase tax revenue. Some of the proposals call for a ceiling on how much an employer can contribute; others call for a floor. The outcome of this debate is by no means certain. Thc guiding principle behind the government's approach is equity—not only between highly compensated and lower-paid employees, but also between employees of companies that offer benefits packages of drastically different values.

-418-

Why does group health insurance enjoy its present tax status?

Group health insurance premiums have enjoyed their tax-free status because of historical and social factors. The benefits of widespread health insurance were obvious to all, and encouraging the growth of health insurance became acceptable social and public policy. Private industry was seen as the most efficient and broad-based way to allow the majority of Americans to receive such benefits. Group health insurance benefits are now seen as an effective way to attract, recruit, and retain superior employees. Therefore, to achieve this social goal, employer contributions to health insurance for employees were accorded their present favorable tax status.

-419-

What would the impact be if the tax status of group health insurance changed?

Changing the tax status of group health insurance would affect both employers and employees. Employees are accustomed to receiving this employee benefit without paying taxes on it; therefore, taxing the benefit might appear to be a "give back." Consequently, employees would demand either additional benefits or cash compensation to make up for this loss. The effect on employers, then, would be an increase in the total compensation offered to employees. Employers might, therefore, be reluctant to offer such benefits to the extent they once did. This, of course, is contrary to the social goal of widespread health insurance. In addition, flexible benefits plans could become even more attractive, since employees would certainly not want to pay taxes on benefits they do not need or want.

-420-

What other legislation will affect health insurance plans?

Recently passed legislation requires employers to offer continued health insurance coverage for up to 36 months to employees and their dependents who lose coverage because of the death of the employee, divorce, attainment of the child age limit, the employee's eligibility for Medicare, or termination of employment. This gives such people continued protection from financial risk. Some or all of the cost can be charged to the insured; the cost of the plan to the employer will increase to the extent of its contributions.

State laws mandating specific coverage for alcoholism, drug abuse, and mental illness have been passed, and will affect the design of group health insurance plans, depending upon the state law that applies. State hospital cost-control legislation and certificate-of-need legislation are designed to help control future costs of health care by regulating allowable hospital charges.

Proposed legislation that prohibits discrimination in benefits or contributions in favor of highly compensated employees must be taken into account in all benefits plan designs. In addition, proposals have been made to change the structure of employer contributions when an HMO is part of a group health insurance plan. This is the result of complaints on the part of employers that the current equal-contribution rule is unfair because employees enrolling in HMOs have been younger and healthier than employees enrolling in traditional indemnity plans.

-421-

What impact will preventive care programs and health risk profiles have on group health insurance?

Preventive care programs and health risk profiles are tools for insurers and employers to pinpoint potential health risks and to encourage healthier life styles. They also lead an employer to implement programs in those areas that cause the greatest risk in the employee population, for example, smoking and obesity. The intended result of such tools and programs is to improve employees' health and decrease medical claims. This, in turn, will lead to lower costs for health care and health insurance.

As the benefits of such tools become apparent to more and more employers, those with healthy employees will be unwilling to subsidize the health care costs of employers with less healthy employees. Insurers may begin to either rate such healthier employee groups on their own (if the employee group is large enough), or pool such employers together to determine lower premium rates that reflect the relative healthiness of their employees and the use of such preventive care programs. As a result, employers that have not adopted such programs or that have employee groups with known but preventable health risks will pay higher premiums, and will be pooled together. Healthier employees may also be unwilling to subsidize the health care costs of less healthy co-workers. It is possible that in the future, employees will pay for their health care based on their own individual health risks.

Appendix

Following are tables showing how the costs of medical care have increased over the past 20 years in different areas of the country. All the tables reflect the consumer price index for medical care, with 1967 equaling 100.

U.S. City Average for All Urban Consumers

Year	*Index*	*% Increase Medical*	*% Increase All Items*
1967	100.0	N/A	N/A
1968	106.1	6.1	4.2
1969	113.4	6.9	5.4
1970	120.6	6.3	5.9
1971	128.4	6.5	4.3
1972	132.5	3.2	3.3
1973	137.7	3.9	6.2
1974	150.5	9.3	11.0
1975	168.6	12.0	9.1
1976	184.7	9.5	5.8
1977	202.4	9.6	6.5
1978	219.4	8.4	7.6
1979	239.7	9.3	11.3
1980	265.9	10.9	13.5
1981	294.5	10.8	10.4
1982	328.7	11.6	6.1
1983	357.3	8.7	3.2
1984	379.5	6.2	4.3
1985	403.1	6.2	3.6

Anchorage, AK

Year	*Index*	*% Increase*
1967	NA	N/A
1968	NA	N/A
1969	NA	N/A
1970	NA	N/A
1971	126.7	N/A
1972	129.2	2.0
1973	134.4	4.0
1974	149.5	11.2
1975	168.9	13.0
1976	189.4	12.1
1977	208.8	10.2
1978	228.6	9.5
1979	249.1	9.0
1980	284.1	14.1
1981	313.1	10.2
1982	341.8	9.2
1983	359.2	5.1
1984	380.3	5.9
1985	399.8	5.1

Atlanta, GA

Year	*Index*	*% Increase*
1967	100.0	N/A
1968	106.7	6.7
1969	117.4	10.0
1970	126.2	7.5
1971	136.1	7.8
1972	139.6	2.6
1973	146.3	4.8
1974	162.4	11.0
1975	183.7	13.1
1976	197.2	7.3
1977	214.0	8.5
1978	224.8	5.0
1979	239.8	6.7
1980	263.3	9.8
1981	290.0	10.0
1982	326.4	12.6
1983	356.5	9.2
1984	374.3	5.0
1985	397.8	6.3

Baltimore, MD

Year	*Index*	*% Increase*
1967	100.0	N/A
1968	105.6	5.6
1969	112.6	6.6
1970	123.1	9.3
1971	135.9	10.4
1972	142.5	4.9
1973	148.9	4.5
1974	165.1	10.9
1975	180.4	9.3
1976	192.8	6.9
1977	207.6	7.7
1978	220.5	6.2
1979	242.1	9.8
1980	265.5	9.7
1981	285.0	7.3
1982	315.3	10.6
1983	337.6	7.1
1984	353.4	4.7
1985	375.2	6.2

Boston, MA

Year	*Index*	*% Increase*
1967	100.0	N/A
1968	108.1	8.1
1969	116.5	7.8
1970	124.4	6.8
1971	130.4	4.8
1972	134.7	3.3
1973	138.9	3.1
1974	148.8	7.1
1975	166.4	11.8
1976	177.5	6.7
1977	192.1	8.2
1978	206.0	7.2
1979	230.8	12.0
1980	255.5	10.7
1981	278.1	8.8
1982	307.7	10.6
1983	328.4	6.7
1984	360.7	9.8
1985	400.3	11.0

Buffalo, NY

Year	*Index*	*% Increase*
1967	100.0	N/A
1968	103.9	3.9
1969	109.0	4.9
1970	115.5	6.0
1971	122.3	5.9
1972	126.1	3.1
1973	130.2	3.3
1974	142.1	9.1
1975	155.3	9.3
1976	168.3	8.4
1977	182.1	8.2
1978	198.3	8.9
1979	212.7	7.3
1980	227.9	7.1
1981	249.1	9.3
1982	266.0	6.8
1983	293.4	10.3
1984	313.0	6.7
1985	328.7	5.0

Chicago, IL

Year	*Index*	*% Increase*
1967	100.0	N/A
1968	105.9	5.9
1969	112.4	6.1
1970	119.9	6.7
1971	128.4	7.1
1972	131.5	2.4
1973	137.0	4.2
1974	150.1	9.6
1975	169.1	12.7
1976	188.7	11.6
1977	207.4	9.9
1978	222.2	7.1
1979	241.7	8.8
1980	272.9	12.9
1981	301.3	10.4
1982	329.4	9.3
1983	361.4	9.7
1984	381.9	5.7
1985	403.3	5.6

Cincinnati, OH

Year	*Index*	*% Increase*
1967	100.0	N/A
1968	107.6	7.6
1969	116.7	5.0
1970	122.5	8.5
1971	131.8	7.6
1972	136.5	3.6
1973	143.8	5.3
1974	158.8	10.4
1975	176.7	11.3
1976	197.0	11.5
1977	220.6	12.0
1978	245.6	11.3
1979	272.1	10.8
1980	296.9	9.1
1981	321.9	8.4
1982	350.6	8.9
1983	375.3	7.0
1984	398.2	6.1
1985	419.8	5.4

Cleveland, OH

Year	*Index*	*% Increase*
1967	100.0	N/A
1968	108.4	8.4
1969	121.4	12.0
1970	130.9	7.8
1971	140.0	7.0
1972	144.0	2.9
1973	150.9	4.8
1974	164.3	8.9
1975	183.0	11.4
1976	201.2	9.9
1977	225.5	12.1
1978	246.0	9.1
1979	262.4	6.7
1980	289.0	10.1
1981	322.6	11.6
1982	363.5	12.7
1983	402.0	10.6
1984	426.8	6.2
1985	444.7	4.2

Dallas—Fort Worth, TX

Year	*Index*	*% Increase*
1967	100.0	N/A
1968	106.1	6.1
1969	114.5	7.9
1970	123.1	7.5
1971	128.8	4.6
1972	131.6	2.2
1973	136.9	4.0
1974	147.7	7.9
1975	162.8	10.2
1976	177.1	8.8
1977	195.3	10.3
1978	210.7	7.9
1979	222.4	5.6
1980	247.3	11.2
1981	284.0	14.8
1982	325.0	14.4
1983	357.9	10.1
1984	378.4	5.7
1985	403.0	6.5

Denver—Boulder, CO

Year	*Index*	*% Increase*
1967	NA	N/A
1968	NA	N/A
1969	NA	N/A
1970	NA	N/A
1971	123.2	N/A
1972	126.8	2.9
1973	131.5	3.7
1974	143.7	9.3
1975	159.7	11.1
1976	172.1	7.8
1977	188.2	9.4
1978	204.6	8.7
1979	223.1	9.0
1980	248.4	11.3
1981	273.0	9.9
1982	307.2	12.5
1983	340.1	10.7
1984	364.1	7.1
1985	388.2	6.6

Detroit, MI

Year	*Index*	*% Increase*
1967	100.0	N/A
1968	106.6	6.6
1969	114.4	7.3
1970	124.4	8.9
1971	134.1	7.8
1972	141.4	5.4
1973	148.5	5.0
1974	162.8	9.6
1975	187.4	15.1
1976	209.4	11.7
1977	234.8	12.1
1978	251.8	7.2
1979	274.5	9.0
1980	297.7	8.5
1981	320.1	7.5
1982	346.4	8.2
1983	365.5	5.5
1984	403.1	10.3
1985	432.5	7.3

Honolulu, HI

Year	*Index*	*% Increase*
1967	100.0	N/A
1968	105.9	5.9
1969	113.2	6.9
1970	118.4	4.6
1971	124.7	5.3
1972	127.5	2.2
1973	133.3	4.5
1974	147.0	10.3
1975	164.8	12.1
1976	182.1	10.5
1977	203.0	11.5
1978	221.0	8.9
1979	238.7	8.0
1980	258.6	8.3
1981	289.4	11.9
1982	324.3	12.1
1983	357.6	10.3
1984	379.7	6.2
1985	400.6	5.5

Houston, TX

Year	*Index*	*% Increase*
1967	100.0	N/A
1968	105.4	5.4
1969	114.7	8.8
1970	122.9	7.1
1971	130.1	5.9
1972	135.3	4.0
1973	140.8	4.1
1974	152.5	8.3
1975	173.7	13.9
1976	192.8	11.0
1977	217.7	13.0
1978	238.8	9.7
1979	261.7	9.6
1980	290.0	10.8
1981	321.7	10.9
1982	362.6	13.3
1983	406.5	11.5
1984	434.6	6.9
1985	469.3	8.0

Kansas City, MO—KS

Year	*Index*	*% Increase*
1967	100.0	N/A
1968	106.5	6.5
1969	112.1	5.3
1970	117.0	4.4
1971	124.4	6.3
1972	129.1	3.8
1973	135.1	4.6
1974	147.7	9.3
1975	160.5	8.7
1976	174.1	8.5
1977	190.9	9.6
1978	208.7	9.3
1979	234.4	12.3
1980	261.1	11.4
1981	293.5	12.4
1982	335.2	14.2
1983	372.4	11.1
1984	397.0	6.6
1985	411.1	3.6

Los Angeles, CA

Year	*Index*	*% Increase*
1967	100.0	N/A
1968	105.5	5.5
1969	111.8	6.0
1970	119.8	7.2
1971	125.7	4.9
1972	128.7	2.4
1973	134.9	4.8
1974	147.7	9.5
1975	165.7	12.2
1976	187.0	12.9
1977	204.2	9.2
1978	222.2	8.8
1979	244.8	10.2
1980	275.6	12.6
1981	310.7	12.7
1982	356.7	12.9
1983	381.8	7.0
1984	398.8	4.5
1985	428.0	7.3

Miami, FL

Year	*Index*	*% Increase*
1967	NA	N/A
1968	NA	N/A
1969	NA	N/A
1970	NA	N/A
1971	NA	N/A
1972	NA	N/A
1973	NA	N/A
1974	NA	N/A
1975	NA	N/A
1976	NA	N/A
1977	NA	N/A
1978	106.1	N/A
1979	119.0	12.2
1980	130.5	9.7
1981	141.4	8.4
1982	162.1	14.6
1983	174.5	7.6
1984	181.6	4.1
1985	188.6	3.9

Milwaukee, WI

Year	*Index*	*% Increase*
1967	100.0	N/A
1968	105.7	5.7
1969	113.1	7.0
1970	119.3	5.5
1971	126.1	5.7
1972	128.1	1.6
1973	134.0	4.6
1974	147.4	10.0
1975	163.6	11.0
1976	182.7	11.7
1977	199.2	9.0
1978	215.2	8.0
1979	240.7	11.8
1980	270.5	12.4
1981	301.3	11.4
1982	325.4	8.0
1983	349.6	7.4
1984	367.2	5.0
1985	379.6	3.4

Minneapolis—St. Paul, MN

Year	*Index*	*% Increase*
1967	100.0	N/A
1968	105.2	5.2
1969	110.4	4.9
1970	117.7	6.6
1971	123.8	5.2
1972	126.0	1.8
1973	132.3	5.0
1974	144.2	9.0
1975	159.6	10.7
1976	171.9	7.7
1977	185.9	8.1
1978	201.0	8.1
1979	217.6	8.3
1980	242.0	11.2
1981	263.9	9.0
1982	295.6	12.0
1983	329.4	11.4
1984	360.5	9.4
1985	384.1	6.5

New York City—Northeastern NJ

Year	*Index*	*% Increase*
1967	100.0	N/A
1968	106.6	6.6
1969	116.6	9.4
1970	125.3	7.5
1971	135.8	8.4
1972	140.2	3.2
1973	145.1	3.5
1974	160.7	10.8
1975	181.0	12.6
1976	199.9	10.4
1977	217.1	8.6
1978	230.2	6.0
1979	248.3	7.9
1980	272.1	9.6
1981	296.7	9.0
1982	323.3	9.0
1983	352.4	9.0
1984	380.8	8.1
1985	408.0	7.1

Northeastern Pennsylvania

Year	*Index*	*% Increase*
1967	100.0	N/A
1968	105.7	5.7
1969	115.8	9.6
1970	121.5	4.9
1971	129.9	6.9
1972	136.8	5.3
1973	140.9	3.0
1974	155.5	10.4
1975	171.2	10.1
1976	183.5	7.2
1977	198.9	8.4
1978	219.6	10.4
1979	236.7	7.8
1980	267.7	13.1
1981	312.2	16.6
1982	352.9	13.0
1983	385.1	9.1
1984	408.8	6.2
1985	440.1	7.7

Philadelphia, PA

Year	*Index*	*% Increase*
1967	100.0	N/A
1968	108.1	8.1
1969	117.4	8.6
1970	127.2	8.3
1971	137.4	8.0
1972	142.1	3.4
1973	149.0	4.9
1974	162.4	9.0
1975	184.3	13.5
1976	200.0	9.0
1977	220.6	9.8
1978	236.5	7.2
1979	255.8	8.2
1980	282.2	10.3
1981	313.7	11.2
1982	343.1	9.4
1983	376.3	9.7
1984	402.7	7.0
1985	445.5	10.6

Pittsburgh, PA

Year	*Index*	*% Increase*
1967	100.0	N/A
1968	105.6	5.6
1969	112.1	6.2
1970	117.7	5.0
1971	122.6	4.2
1972	128.7	5.0
1973	134.2	4.3
1974	147.0	9.5
1975	162.9	10.8
1976	179.5	10.2
1977	198.5	10.6
1978	215.9	8.8
1979	239.0	10.7
1980	265.0	10.9
1981	296.9	12.0
1982	333.6	12.4
1983	375.7	12.6
1984	408.0	8.6
1985	422.3	3.5

Portland, OR

Year	*Index*	*% Increase*
1967	100.0	N/A
1968	105.2	5.2
1969	111.4	5.9
1970	118.7	6.6
1971	123.3	3.9
1972	127.5	3.4
1973	135.6	6.5
1974	149.4	10.2
1975	166.0	11.1
1976	180.7	8.9
1977	199.1	10.2
1978	217.2	9.1
1979	237.7	9.4
1980	268.1	12.8
1981	300.4	12.0
1982	337.6	12.4
1983	363.0	7.5
1984	381.6	5.1
1985	401.2	5.1

San Diego, CA

Year	*Index*	*% Increase*
1967	100.0	N/A
1968	102.6	2.6
1969	108.0	5.3
1970	114.8	6.3
1971	121.0	5.4
1972	123.8	2.3
1973	130.1	5.1
1974	143.9	10.6
1975	161.5	12.2
1976	178.5	10.5
1977	195.3	9.4
1978	211.8	8.4
1979	231.7	9.4
1980	253.8	9.5
1981	276.6	9.0
1982	310.3	12.2
1983	335.6	8.2
1984	353.8	5.4
1985	366.9	3.7

San Francisco—Oakland, CA

Year	*Index*	*% Increase*
1967	100.0	N/A
1968	104.9	4.9
1969	110.1	5.0
1970	116.1	5.4
1971	123.1	6.0
1972	127.1	3.2
1973	132.0	3.9
1974	143.5	8.7
1975	164.9	14.9
1976	181.6	10.1
1977	199.7	10.0
1978	218.7	9.5
1979	238.9	9.2
1980	264.6	10.8
1981	292.3	10.5
1982	325.6	11.4
1983	348.2	6.9
1984	363.1	4.3
1985	384.1	5.8

Seattle—Everett, WA

Year	*Index*	*% Increase*
1967	100.0	N/A
1968	105.9	5.9
1969	113.1	6.8
1970	118.4	4.7
1971	122.9	3.8
1972	125.5	2.1
1973	129.9	3.5
1974	141.6	9.0
1975	158.5	11.9
1976	175.0	10.4
1977	192.3	9.9
1978	213.6	11.1
1979	231.7	8.5
1980	260.6	12.5
1981	291.6	11.9
1982	321.3	10.2
1983	346.8	7.9
1984	362.9	4.6
1985	385.6	6.3

St. Louis, MO

Year	*Index*	*% Increase*
1967	100.0	N/A
1968	104.8	4.8
1969	111.2	6.1
1970	118.4	6.5
1971	123.5	4.3
1972	125.8	1.9
1973	129.9	3.3
1974	140.8	8.4
1975	155.9	10.7
1976	168.9	8.3
1977	186.7	10.5
1978	200.8	7.6
1979	218.1	8.6
1980	245.5	12.6
1981	275.4	12.2
1982	314.4	14.2
1983	339.6	8.0
1984	356.1	4.9
1985	373.8	5.0

Washington, D.C.—MD—VA

Year	*Index*	*% Increase*
1967	100.0	N/A
1968	109.4	9.4
1969	117.9	7.8
1970	127.0	7.7
1971	136.5	7.5
1972	139.9	2.5
1973	144.4	3.2
1974	161.1	11.6
1975	179.5	11.4
1976	197.6	10.1
1977	215.9	9.3
1978	230.3	6.7
1979	252.7	9.7
1980	274.8	8.7
1981	296.6	7.9
1982	335.4	13.1
1983	375.8	12.0
1984	399.3	6.3
1985	424.5	6.3

List of State Insurance Commissioners

Following is a list (alphabetical by state) of state commissioners of insurance and their addresses, telephone numbers, and office hours, from the American Council of Life Insurance.

Alabama

Michael DeBellis, Commissioner of Insurance
135 South Union Street
Montgomery, Alabama 36130
Phone: (205) 269-3550
(205) 269-3554
Office hours: 8:00–5:00

Alaska

John L. George, Director of Insurance
Department of Commerce
Division of Insurance, Pouch "D"
Juneau, Alaska 99811
Phone: (907) 465-2515

3601 "C" Street
Suite 722
Anchorage, Alaska 99503
Phone: (907) 562-3626
Office hours: 8:00–4:30

Arizona

David Childers, Director of Insurance
801 East Jefferson
Phoenix, Arizona 85034-2217
Phone: (602) 255-5400
(602) 255-1986
Office hours: 8:00–5:00

Arkansas

Robert M. Eubanks III, Insurance Commissioner
400-18 University Tower Building
Little Rock, Arkansas 72204
Phone: (501) 371-1325
Office hours: 8:00–5:00

California

Bruce Bunner, Insurance Commissioner
100 Van Ness Avenue
San Francisco, California 94102
Phone: (415) 557-1126

600 South Commonwealth Avenue
Los Angeles, California 90005
Phone: (213) 736-2572
Office hours: 8:00–5:00

Colorado

John Kezer, Commissioner of Insurance
303 West Colfax Avenue
Fifth Floor
Denver, Colorado 80204
Phone: (303) 573-3410
Office hours: 8:00–5:00

Connecticut

Peter W. Gillies, Insurance Commissioner
165 Capitol Avenue
Hartford, Connecticut 06106
Phone: (203) 566-5275
Office hours: 8:30–4:30

Delaware

David N. Levinson, Insurance Commissioner
21 The Green
Dover, Delaware 19901
Phone: (302) 736-4251
Office hours: 8:00–4:30

District of Columbia

Margurite C. Stokes, Superintendent of Insurance (Acting)
North Potomac Building
614 H Street, N.W., Room 512
Washington, D.C. 20001
Phone: (202) 727-7419
Office hours: 8:15–4:45

Florida

Bill Gunter, Commissioner of Insurance
and Treasurer
Larson Building
Tallahassee, Florida 32301
Phone: (904) 488-3440
Office hours: 8:00–5:00

Georgia

Warren D. Evans, Insurance Commissioner
7th Floor, West Floyd Tower
200 Piedmont Avenue, S.E.
Atlanta, Georgia 30334
Phone: (404) 656-2056
Office hours: 8:00–4:30

Hawaii

Mario R. Ramil, Insurance Commissioner
Department of Commerce & Consumer Affairs,
Insurance Division
P.O. Box 3614
Honolulu, Hawaii 96811
Phone: (808) 548-6522
Office hours: 7:45–4:30

Idaho

Wayne L. Soward, Director of Insurance
700 West State Street
Boise, Idaho 83720
Phone: (208) 334-2250
Office hours: 8:00–5:00

Illinois

John E. Washburn, Director
320 West Washington Street
Springfield, Illinois 62767
Phone: (217) 782-4515
Office hours: 8:00–4:30

160 North LaSalle Street
Chicago, Illinois 60601
Phone: (312) 917-2420

Indiana

Harry E. Eakin, Commissioner of Insurance
509 State Office Building
Indianapolis, Indiana 46204
Phone: (317) 232-2385
Office hours: 8:00–4:30

Iowa

Bruce W. Foudree, Commissioner
Lucas State Office Building
Des Moines, Iowa 50319
Phone: (515) 281-5705
Office hours: 8:00–4:30

Kansas

Fletcher Bell, Commissioner of Insurance
420 S.W. 9th Street
Topeka, Kansas 66612
Phone: (913) 296-3071
Office hours: 8:00–5:00

Kentucky

Gil McCarty, Commissioner of Insurance
P.O. Box 517
229 West Main Street
Frankfort, Kentucky 40602
Phone: (502) 564-3630
Office hours: 8:00–4:30

Louisiana

Sherman A. Bernard, Commissioner of Insurance
State Insurance Building
P.O. Box 44214
Capitol Station
Baton Rouge, Louisiana 70804
Phone: (504) 342-5322
(504) 342-5348
Office hours: 8:00–4:30

Maine

Theodore T. Briggs, Superintendent
State House Station 34
Augusta, Maine 04333
Phone: (207) 289-3101
Office hours: 8:00–5:00

Maryland

Edward J. Muhl, Insurance Commissioner
501 St. Paul Place
Baltimore, Maryland 21202
Phone: (301) 659-4027
Office hours: 8:30–4:30

Massachusetts

Peter Hiam, Commissioner of Insurance
Department of Banking and Insurance,
Division of Insurance
100 Cambridge Street
Boston, Massachusetts 02202
Phone: (617) 727-3333
Office hours: 8:45–5:00

Michigan
Herman W. Coleman, Insurance Commissioner
Department of Licensing and Regulation
P.O. Box 30220
100 North Pine Street
Lansing, Michigan 48909
Phone: (517) 373-0220
(517) 373-9273
Office hours: 8:00-5:00

Minnesota
Michael A. Hatch, Commissioner of Insurance
Department of Commerce
5th Floor Metro Square Building
7th and Robert Streets
St. Paul, Minnesota, 55101
Phone: (612) 296-2594
(612) 296-6848
Office hours: 8:00-4:30

Mississippi
George Dale, Commissioner of Insurance
Department of Insurance
P.O. Box 79
Jackson, Mississippi 39205
Phone: (601) 359-3569
Office hours: 8:00-5:00

Missouri
Lewis R. Crist, Director of Insurance
Missouri Division of Insurance
P. O. Box 690
Jefferson City, Missouri 65102
Phone: (314) 751-4126
Office hours: 8:00-5:00

Montana
Andrea Bennett, State Auditor & Commissioner of Insurance
Department of Insurance
Sam W. Mitchell Building
Helena, Montana 59601
Phone: (406) 444-2040
Office hours: 8:00-5:00

Nebraska
Michael J. Dugan, Director of Insurance
Department of Insurance
P.O. Box 94699
301 Centennial Mall South
Lincoln, Nebraska 68509
Phone: (402) 471-2201
Office hours: 8:00-5:00

Nevada

David A. Gates, Commissioner of Insurance
Division of Insurance
Nye Building
201 S. Fall Street
Carson City, Nevada
Phone: (702) 386-4270

New Hampshire

Louis E. Bergeron, Insurance Commissioner
Department of Insurance
GAA Plaza
169 Manchester Street
Concord, New Hampshire 03301
Phone: (603) 271-2261 through 2267
Office hours: 8:00–4:30

New Jersey

Hazel Cluck, Commissioner of Insurance
Department of Insurance
201 East State Street
CN-325
Trenton, New Jersey 08625
Phone: (609) 292-6812
Office hours: 8:30–5:00

New Mexico

Vicente B. Jasso, Superintendent of Insurance
Department of Insurance
P.O. Box 11269
Santa Fe, New Mexico 87503
Phone: (505) 827-4535
Office hours: 8:00–5:00

New York

James P. Corcoran, Superintendent of Insurance
Department of Insurance
106 West Broadway
New York, New York 10013
Phone: (212) 602-0428
Office hours: 8:45–5:00

Agency Building One
Nelson A. Rockefeller Plaza
Albany, New York 12257
Phone: (518) 474-6600
Office hours: 8:30–4:30

North Carolina
James E. Long, Commissioner of Insurance
Department of Insurance
P.O. Box 26387
Dobbs Building
Raleigh, North Carolina 27611
Phone: (919) 733-7343
Office hours: 8:00–5:00

North Dakota
Earl R. Pomeroy, Commissioner of Insurance
Department of Insurance
State Capitol—Fifth Floor
Bismarck, North Dakota 58505-0158
Phone: (701) 224-2440
Office hours: 8:00–12:00; 1:00–5:00

Ohio
George Fabe, Director of Insurance
Department of Insurance
2100 Stella Court
Columbus, Ohio 43215
Phone: (614) 466-3584
Office hours: 8:00–5:00

Oklahoma
Gerald Grimes, State Insurance Commissioner
Department of Insurance
408 Will Rogers Memorial Office Building
Oklahoma City, Oklahoma 73105
Phone: (405) 521-2828
Office hours: 7:45–4:30

Oregon
Josephine M. Driscoll, Commissioner
Insurance Division
158-12th Street, N.E.
Salem, Oregon 97310
Phone: (503) 378-4271
Office hours: 8:00–5:00

Pennsylvania
George F. Grode, Commissioner of Insurance
Department of Insurance
13th Floor, Strawberry Square
Harrisburg, Pennsylvania 17120
Phone: (717) 787-5173
Office hours: 8:00–4:30

Puerto Rico

Juan Antonio Garcia, Commissioner of Insurance
Office of the Commissioner of Insurance
P.O. Box 8330
Fernandez Juncos Station
Santurce, Puerto Rico 00910
Phone: (809) 724-6565
Office hours: 8:00–4:30

Rhode Island

Clifton A. Moore, Insurance Commissioner
Insurance Division
100 North Main Street
Providence, Rhode Island 02903
Phone: (401) 277-2223
Office hours: 8:30–4:30

South Carolina

John G. Richards, Chief Insurance Commissioner
Department of Insurance
2711 Middleburg Drive
Columbia, South Carolina 29204
Phone: (803) 758-3266
Office hours: 8:30–5:00

South Dakota

Susan L. Walker, Director of Insurance
Division of Insurance
Insurance Building
320 N. Nicollet
Pierre, South Dakota 57501
Phone: (605) 773-3563
Office hours: 8:00–5:00

Tennessee

John C. Neff, Commissioner of Insurance
Department of Commerce and Insurance
1808 W. End Avenue
Nashville, Tennessee 37219-5318
Phone: (615) 741-2241
Office hours: 8:00–4:30

Texas

Doyce R. Lee, Commissioner of Insurance
1110 San Jacinto
Austin, Texas 78701-1998
Phone: (512) 463-6169 (Information)
(512) 463-6332
Office hours: 8:00–5:00

Utah
Harold C. Yancey, Commissioner of Insurance
Department of Insurance
Heber M. Wells Building
160 East 300 South, P.O. Box 45803
Salt Lake City, Utah 84145
Phone: (801) 530-6400
Office hours: 8:00–5:00

Vermont
David T. Bard, Commissioner of Insurance
Division of Insurance
Department of Banking & Insurance,
State Office Building
Montpelier, Vermont 05602
Phone: (802) 828-3301
Office hours: 7:45–4:30

Virginia
James M. Thomson, Commissioner of Insurance
Bureau of Insurance
State Corporation Commission
P.O. Box 1157
Richmond, Virginia 23209
Phone: (804) 786-3741
Office hours: 8:15–5:00

Washington
Dick Marquardt, Insurance Commissioner
and State Fire Marshal
Department of Insurance
Insurance Building AQ-21
Olympia, Washington 98504
Phone: (206) 753-7300
Office hours: 8:00–5:00

West Virginia
Fred E. Wright, Insurance Commissioner
Department of Insurance
2100 Washington Street East
Charleston, West Virginia 25305
Phone: (304) 348-3354
Office hours: 8:30–4:30

Wisconsin
Thomas P. Fox, Commissioner of Insurance
Office of the Commissioner of Insurance
P.O. Box 7873
123 West Washington Ave.
Madison, Wisconsin 53707
Phone: (608) 266-3585
(608) 266-0102
Office hours: 7:45–4:30

Wyoming

Robert W. Schrader, Insurance Commissioner
Department of Insurance
122 West 25th Street
Herschler Building
Cheyenne, Wyoming 82002-0440
Phone: (307) 777-7401
Office hours: 8:00–5:00

Glossary of Acronyms

Following is a list of acronyms (arranged in alphabetical order) that appear in the text. Each item is spelled out and briefly defined to facilitate the readers' use of this book.

AD&D (Accidental Death and Dismemberment): One of the four major components of health insurance coverage employers provide their employees. The others are: life, disability, and medical insurance. AD&D provides coverage for death or dismemberment resulting directly from accidental causes.

ADEA (Age Discrimination in Employment Act of 1967): As amended in 1978, ADEA requires employers with 200 or more employees to offer older active employees under age 70 who are eligible for Medicare (and their spouses if they are also under age 70) the same health insurance coverage that is provided to younger employees.

ASO (Administrative Services Only): An ASO plan is a contract from an insurer to provide a fully self-insured employer with administrative services only.

BC/BS (Blue Cross/Blue Shield): The Blues provide nonprofit health insurance to millions of Americans. Operating at the state and city level, the Blues dominate third-party insurance reimbursement in many geographic areas because of their ability to offer reduced rates through negotiated discounts with health care providers.

COB (Coordination of Benefits): COB is a cost-control mechanism to prevent an employee from receiving duplicate benefits from two or more insurers.

CSO (Claims Services Only): A CSO plan is a contract designed for fully self-insured employers that need very little administrative assistance. Under a CSO arrangement, the insurer administers only the claims portion of the plan.

DEFRA (Deficit Reduction Act of 1984): DEFRA helps prevent discrimination against elderly employees in health insurance, particularly in regard to extending the provisions of TEFRA. It requires group health plans to be offered to employees' dependents in the 65–69 age bracket, even if the employees are not in that age bracket.

DRGs (Diagnosis-Related Groups): DRGs are used to determine the amount Medicare reimburses each hospital that provides its insureds with service, as part of its prospective payment system. Each DRG corresponds to a patient condition. DRGs were developed at Yale University in 1975.

E of I (Evidence of Insurability): Insurers require E of I, or proof of an individual's health condition, to determine whether insurance will be granted.

EOB (Explanation of Benefits): An EOB is a document that accompanies a claims check. It summarizes how reimbursement was determined and, among other things, explains the claims appeal process.

EPO (Exclusive Provider Organization): An EPO is a more rigid type of PPO that requires the employee to use only designated providers or sacrifice reimbursement altogether. PPOs encourage employees to use "preferred" providers through more generous reimbursement, but will still reimburse for nonpreferred providers.

ERISA (Employee Retirement Income Security Act of 1974): Primarily enacted to effect pension equality, ERISA also contains provisions to protect the interests of group insurance plan participants and beneficiaries. It requires, among other things, that insurance plans be established pursuant to a written instrument that describes the benefits provided under the plan, names the persons responsible for the operation of the plan, and spells out the arrangements for funding and amending the plan.

FMCs (Foundations for Medical Care): A forerunner program to utilization review, these watchdog organizations were established in the early 1960s for recipients of Medicare.

HMO (Health Maintenance Organization): An HMO is an organization that, for a prepaid fee, provides comprehensive health care services to a voluntarily enrolled membership. HMOs are sponsored by large employers, labor unions, medical schools, hospitals, medical clinics, and even insurance companies. Development of HMOs was spurred by the federal government in the 1970s as a means to correct the structural, inflationary problems with conventional health care payment.

HRA (Health Risk Appraisal): A survey used by employers to determine the likelihood of an insured experiencing death, illness, or injury in the future. It helps employers decide whether wellness and other preventive care programs are necessary.

HSID (High Self-Insured Deductible): HSID is a way for employers to improve cash flow by self-funding the first tier of any employee's health care expenses. Employers can thus retain funds that would normally be paid to the insurance company to cover current and future claims.

IBNR (Incurred But Not Reported): Claims that have been incurred but have not been reported to the insurer as of some specific date.

IPA Model (Individual Practice Association Model): One of the four different models by which HMOs are organized. The others are the group model, the network model, and the staff model. The IPA model is a mixture of physicians from solo and group practices.

MET (Multiple Employer Trust): A MET is a mechanism that allows small employers in the same or a related industry to provide affordable, quality group insurance to their employees under a trust arrangement. Without a MET, these companies would be unable to purchase group insurance. A MET is most common among employers with 10 or fewer employees.

MPP (Minimum Premium Plan): An MPP is another way of self-funding to improve cash flow, whereby the employer assumes responsibility for funding most benefits and the insurer assumes liability for benefits above a predetermined level. As under HSID, the premiums are reduced significantly under an MPP.

OASDI (Old Age, Survivors' and Disability Insurance Act): The 1965 amendment to OASDI established Medicare, effective July 1966.

OOP Maximum (Out-of-Pocket maximum): OOP maximum refers to the maximum amount that an insured employee will have to pay for expenses covered under the plan. It is usually $500 or $1,000.

PAT (Preadmission Testing): PAT is a cost-control mechanism intended to reduce hospital stays by encouraging employees to have routine hospital testing done on an outpatient basis before being admitted to the hospital. Reimbursement is sometimes made on a more generous basis for PAT.

PPA (Preferred Provider Arrangement): A PPA differs from a PPO in that it is an agreement between providers and another entity, whereas a PPO is an organization of providers.

PPO (Preferred Provider Organization): A health care provider arrangement whereby a third-party payer contracts with a group of medical care providers that agrees to furnish services at negotiated fees in return for prompt payment and a guaranteed patient volume. PPOs control costs by keeping fees down and curbing excessive service through stringent utilization control.

PPS (Prospective Payment System): A standardized payment system implemented in 1983 by Medicare to help manage health care reimbursement whereby the incentive for hospitals to deliver unnecessary care is eliminated. Hospitals can expect a fixed reimbursement based not on the number and kinds of services delivered but on the diagnosis of the patient.

PSROs (Professional Standards Review Organizations): The successors of FMCs; 200 of these watchdog organizations were created to provide for review of all federally financed patient care in acute care hospitals.

R&C Charge (Reasonable and Customary Charge): R&C charge refers to the maximum amount an insurer will reimburse for medical care expenses covered under group health insurance plans. Insurers use R&C charges to control health care costs.

SPD (Summary Plan Description): An SPD contains specific information about the health plan. Each plan participant and the Department of Labor must be provided with an SPD.

SSO (Second Surgical Opinion): SSO is a cost-control mechanism to reduce unnecessary surgery by encouraging individuals to seek a second opinion for elective surgery.

TEFRA (Tax Equity and Fiscal Responsibility Act of 1982): TEFRA was enacted to prevent discrimination against elderly employees with regard to health insurance. It amended the Social Security Act to make Medicare secondary to employer group health plans for active employees and spouses aged 65 through 69. TEFRA also amended ADEA to require employers to offer employees and dependents aged 65 through 69 the same coverage available to younger employees.

TLR (Tolerable Loss Ratio): The TLR is the loss ratio the insurer can fund without losing money on the group.

TPA (Third-Party Administrator): TPA refers to a person or organization that provides certain administrative services to group benefits plans, including premium accounting, claims review and payment, claims utilization review, maintenance of employee eligibility records, and negotiations with insurers that provide stop-loss protection for large claims.

UR (Utilization Review): A cost-control mechanism used by some insurers and employers in recent years that evaluates health care on the basis of appropriateness, necessity, and quality. For hospital review, it can include preadmission certification, concurrent review with discharge planning, and retrospective review.

VEBA (Voluntary Employees' Beneficiary Association): A VEBA, also known as a 501(c)(9) trust, is a method of funding an employee benefits plan. It is used almost exclusively by large employers.

Index

(References in the index are to Question Numbers.)